Equipped to Serve

How Seminary Strengthens You for Ministry

"This is a splendid collection of essays on the indispensable role of education in the life of the church and the ways in which seminaries can step in to provide essential tools for pastors and church leaders. Much wisdom here—compassion and conviction, the theoretical and the practical, passion and maturity."

—**TREVIN WAX,** vice president of resources and marketing, North American Mission Board (NAMB); visiting professor at Cedarville University, Ohio; and author of *The Thrill of Orthodoxy, This Is Our Time*, and *Gospel Centered Teaching*

"Critics often claim, 'They never taught me this at seminary.' That's often more an admission a person wasn't paying attention than an accurate critique of seminary curriculum! Seminaries provide wide-ranging, foundational training for ministry leadership—as described in these chapters. Seminary training also provides the framework for addressing new ministry challenges—many unknown to previous generations of church leaders. Seminaries are the seedbed from which long-term, healthy ministry can grow. *Equipped to Serve* makes the case for investing years of preparation for decades of service—a price worth paying as you consider a lifetime of kingdom leadership."

—**JEFF IORG,** president, SBC Executive Committee; former president, Gateway Seminary, Ontario, California

"Reflecting on the three decades that have passed since I walked across the chapel stage at Southern Seminary and was awarded the Master of Divinity degree, I realize now more than ever how formative those years of study were for me. *Equipped to Serve* resonated strongly with me because, as Pace and Six argue, 'Theological education is ministry preparation.' I highly commend their valuable work to help this generation of students maximize the opportunity to prepare for an effective ministry."

—**PAUL CHITWOOD,** president, International Mission Board

"*Equipped to Serve* highlights how Southern Baptist seminaries are uniquely positioned to train God-called leaders for success in ministry. With a commitment to biblical authority, theological depth, and practical ministry preparation, these seminaries don't just fill your mind with knowledge—they shape your heart for service. R. Scott Pace and Jonathan D. Six remind us that seminaries are more than academic institutions; they are Great Commission training grounds that prepare leaders to make an eternal impact."

—**SHANE PRUITT,** director, National Next Gen, North American Mission Board (NAMB); coauthor of *Calling Out the Called: Discipling Those Called to Ministry Leadership*

Equipped to Serve

How Seminary Strengthens You for Ministry

Edited by

R. Scott Pace and Jonathan D. Six

LEXHAM PRESS

Equipped to Serve: How Seminary Strengthens You for Ministry

Lexham Press, 1313 Commercial St., Bellingham, WA 98225
LexhamPress.com

Print ISBN 9781683598824
Digital ISBN 9781683599241

Lexham Editorial: Todd Hains, Elliot Ritzema, Abigail Stocker
Cover Design: Gabriel Eason
Typesetting: Anna Fejes, Mandi Newell

25 26 27 28 29 30 31 / US / 12 11 10 9 8 7 6 5 4 3 2 1

To the memory of Dr. Jim Shaddix, a faithful shepherd, passionate preacher, and devoted mentor. His unwavering commitment to expository preaching through seminary education shaped countless pastors and churches, leaving a legacy of biblical faithfulness and gospel clarity. His voice may be silent, but his impact echoes through the pulpits he influenced. May this work honor his dedication to the Word of God and inspire others to proclaim Christ with the same conviction.

CONTENTS

INTRODUCTION: WHY THEOLOGICAL EDUCATION FOR MINISTRY PREPARATION

R. Scott Pace and Jonathan D. Six

The tides are turning in the church. The average age of pastors and churchgoers is rising.[1] This points to either a massive shortage of pastors or a seismic shift in leadership of evangelical churches. Likely, there has not been a more crucial time to call, train, and send servants of the church than today. This book is about preparing those whom God calls for the work of ministry, which—according to Scripture—includes every Christian. Consider Paul's teaching in Ephesians 4:11–12. God "gave the apostles, the prophets, the evangelists, the shepherds and teachers, to equip the saints for the work of ministry."[2] Paul's implication here is that all believers would do the "work of ministry," while he also identifies the responsibility of leaders designated "to equip" them. While Scripture affirms the broader understanding of ministry that involves all believers, it also presents a narrower rendering for the work of ministry. For

1. Aaron Earls, "Average U.S. Pastor and Churchgoer Grow Old," *Lifeway Research*, https://research.lifeway.com/2021/11/01/americas-pastors-and-churchgoers-are-getting-older/.

2. Scripture references in this chapter are from the English Standard Version.

example, God instructs Timothy and Titus to appoint elders to shepherd and give oversight to the church. This specification of ministry constricts the understanding to an office or position of leadership within the congregation. All believers need and can benefit from theological training, but those who seek to serve the church in a vocational sense should strongly consider formal theological education. This book is a resource for every Christian who is considering theological education but especially for those who are seeking to serve the church in this vocational sense.

Theological education is ministry preparation and is central to the task of a seminary, especially one rooted in the Southern Baptist tradition. Seminaries are tasked with training and mobilizing God-called men and women to serve the church and fulfill the Great Commission. There will be much more to say about calling in chapter 1, but we believe the church must recover an emphasis on calling, training, and sending congregants to serve the church and to do the work of ministry if the church is to flourish in the days ahead and persist in God's Great Commission.

Scripture repeatedly emphasizes the importance of theological and ministerial training. Paul challenged Timothy as a young church leader to be "a good servant of Christ Jesus, being trained in the words of the faith and of the good doctrine" (1 Tim 4:6). He also exhorted him as a young minister to "keep a close watch on yourself and on the teaching" (1 Tim 4:16) and to diligently study and prepare to faithfully handle "the word of truth" (2 Tim 2:15). Likewise, he instructed Titus that church leaders must be "able to give instruction in sound doctrine" and to "teach what accords with sound doctrine" (Titus 1:9, 2:1).

Although these passages do not specifically speak to formal education, they do stress the importance of being theologically trained for the work of ministry. Immersing ourselves in the Scriptures and in ministry practices (1 Tim 4:15), commending ourselves to teachers who can train us to instruct others (2 Tim 2:2), and devoting ourselves to the rigorous preparation that teaching requires (Col 1:29) are all essential aspects of our calling. They also all describe the model and role of theological education!

As you consider your calling, there is also a stewardship aspect that you must consider. You cannot neglect the gifts God has entrusted to you; they cannot remain undiscerned or underdeveloped (1 Tim 4:14; 1 Pet 4:10). Likewise, your spiritual appetite cannot remain immature, your handling of the Scriptures unskilled (1 Tim 3:1), and your doctrinal understanding rudimentary (Heb 5:12–6:1). Admittedly, discipleship and spiritual growth in these areas is primarily the local church's responsibility. While spiritual maturity and ministry preparation does not require formal academic training, educational institutions can serve the church by providing instructional resources that most local churches are not equipped to offer.

This is why a season of theological and ministerial preparation is important. Together, they can help you fulfill your stewardship and spiritual responsibilities as you train for ministry and pursue your calling—ultimately equipping you to serve the Lord by being "rooted and built up in him and established in the faith" (Col 2:6–7).

HOW GOD USES SEASONS OF PREPARATION

God's calling on your life requires a season of preparation. Often people who are enthusiastic about their calling and eager to serve can view a dedicated time for training as an unnecessary delay or interruption in God's plan. But these times are an essential part of our development that the Lord uses to equip us with the knowledge, skills, experience, and faith we need to accomplish his will. For these seasons to serve God's purpose, it is important for Christians to recognize their value and embrace the developmental elements they include. While everyone's spiritual journey and season of formation is unique, God uses periods of ministry preparation to grow us and ready us to serve effectively.

One way God uses seasons of preparation is for *self-development*. Consider the lives of those who were called by God in Scripture. It is easy for us to focus on their triumphs and overlook the intense preparation involved.[3] For example, God's call of Abraham included the promise of a family and nation that would not begin until Isaac was born twenty-five years later. Likewise, the Lord revealed his plan to Joseph as a teenager, but his dreams and God's promises were not fulfilled until he was reunited with his family more than twenty years later. His season of training included family betrayal, enslavement, false accusations, and imprisonment, but God used those experiences to equip him and shape his character (Ps 105:19).

God's plan for Moses was evident by his supernatural protection of him as a child, but he would spend forty years in Midian as a shepherd before God sent him back to Egypt to deliver his people. David was a teenager when Samuel anointed him as king, but he did not ascend to the throne until almost fifteen years later—after he had served as a shepherd, defeated Goliath, suffered banishment, fled through the desert, and fought numerous battles. Similarly, after his dramatic conversion, Paul spent fourteen years exploring his calling as a

3. For a more thorough discussion on preparation for ministry and expanded thoughts on previously published portions of this chapter, please see chapter 11 in R. Scott Pace and Shane Pruitt, *Calling Out the Called* (Nashville: B&H, 2022).

bivocational preacher prior to his first missionary journey as part of God's call to global missions. Even Jesus, who clearly understood his divine purpose at age twelve, did not begin his full-time public ministry until he was thirty!

When you reflect on these testimonies and what God's servants endured, you can understand why some Christians would rather skip the process or run from their call to ministry altogether! However, it is important to notice in these stories how God worked during seasons of preparation to deepen their faith, refine their character, develop their skills, and strengthen their resolve. Those seasons were necessary, and they remind us that *in God's plan, waiting time is never wasted time!* Our self-development involves life experiences that shape our perspective, refine our sense of calling, and promote our overall maturity. These elements will be invaluable as you navigate the various circumstances and challenges in your ministry and as you learn to serve God's people. When we are mindful of our self-development, we can embrace seasons of preparation and commit ourselves to the steps of obedience they require.

God also uses seasons of preparation for *skill development*. When you come to faith in Christ, the Holy Spirit equips you with spiritual gifts that are central components of your calling (1 Pet 4:10–11). Discerning and developing your gifts requires time and effort to clarify your understanding and sharpen your related skills so that you can use them effectively. Seasons of preparation also provide you with the opportunity to serve and volunteer in various ministry contexts and capacities so that you can grow in your spiritual gifts and skills for ministry.

Most important, God uses seasons of preparation for *our spiritual development*. In each of the biblical examples referenced earlier, the Lord was not just giving these leaders time to physically and emotionally mature; he was spiritually maturing them as well. In his waiting, Abraham learned how to trust in God's faithfulness and sovereignty after multiple futile attempts to manipulate his circumstances to accomplish God's plan. Joseph learned how to endure undeserved suffering while remaining hopeful and faithful through perseverance. Moses learned how to overcome guilt, fear, and his own insecurities to trust God's powerful and providential hand of deliverance. David learned how to shepherd God's people by trusting the chief shepherd; how to conquer God's enemies by faith in the divine warrior; and how to lead God's people by submitting himself to the eternal king. Similarly, Paul learned how to trust in God's transforming grace for salvation and sanctification while surrendering his life for the gospel mission.

In the same way, God desires to work in our lives through seasons and situations that mature and strengthen our faith. To harvest the fruit of righteousness that these seasons produce, we must embrace them as times of training and endure them even when they are more painful than pleasant (Gal 6:9; Heb 12:11). Too often we are quick to look for an escape hatch at the first sign of adversity. We would rather avoid the heat of the crucible and the shaping of the anvil. When we do, we circumvent God's sanctifying work in our lives by short-circuiting his immediate plans and forfeiting his future blessings.

Understanding the refining and renewing purpose of these seasons of preparation enables you to embrace them with joy and confidence. Doing so can also accelerate God's work in your life, while resisting them can prolong the process. There are several principles you can adopt to help you grow through the seasons of preparation. First, *learn how to trust God and walk prayerfully* (Phil 4:6–7; Col 4:2). Focus on cultivating a heart of dependence on the Lord through prayer while maintaining faithfulness through obedience. A healthy prayer life helps to relieve the current pressure of preparation and will equip you to navigate challenging seasons throughout your life and ministry (Phil 4:6–7). Second, *learn how to trust God and wait patiently*. Scripture is full of exhortations to "wait" on the Lord (Ps 27:14), but it is a lot easier read than done. Seasons of preparation often involve anonymity, loneliness, and pruning, which make waiting even more difficult. However, as God grows your faith through these times, you can be "joyful in hope, patient in affliction, and faithful in prayer" (Rom 12:12 NIV). Finally, *learn how to trust God to work providentially*. God is always faithful, causing all things to work together for your good and for his glory (Rom 8:28; Gen 50:20). He orchestrates circumstances and experiences to equip you to accomplish his plan. Even though you may not be able to see the outcome of your current situation, you can be confident that he is actively working to accomplish his will in and through your life.

HOW GOD USES SEMINARY FOR PREPARATION

Seasons of ministry preparation often include preparation in seminary. Unfortunately, there are a lot of misconceptions when it comes to seminary. Some people dismiss it as unnecessary and accuse it of being completely detached from real-world ministry. Others avoid it because of the potential pitfall of pride that knowledge can promote (1 Cor 8:1). Meanwhile, some minimize its value as a worldly standard or believe that they can achieve the same level of training on their own.

While a seminary education may not be required for ministry, it can provide invaluable training when approached correctly, both by the institution and by the students. That training can promote spiritual growth and ministry excellence that honors the Lord, serves his church, and fulfills his mission. To accomplish the intended purpose of a seminary education, there are several essential characteristics the student and seminary must possess.

First, *your seminary education should be spiritual.* In ministry, it is easy to mistake dedication for devotion. Your practical responsibilities and your desire to perform them in a professional manner can shift your approach to ministry to become more of a career than a calling. Your ministry can subtly begin to be more of an occupation with obligations instead of obedience with opportunities. In other words, it becomes more about the job than it is about Jesus. In the same way, seminary can easily cause you to be more focused on learning about the Lord instead of loving the Lord, about studying Christ rather than serving Christ.

But these are not mutually exclusive. Just because something is intellectual does not mean that it is unspiritual. The first and greatest commandment calls us to *love* God with all our heart, all our soul, and all our *mind* (Matt 22:37). Likewise, our *spiritual* act of worship and being transformed into the likeness of Christ requires the renewing of our *minds* (Rom 12:1–2). We are called to "grow in the grace and knowledge of our Lord and Savior Jesus Christ" (2 Pet 3:18) as we arm ourselves to discern and dismantle the thoughts and arguments that oppose "the knowledge of God" (2 Cor 10:5).

This means that learning must be leveraged for spiritual depth in your relationship with the Lord. Knowing Christ must be elevated as your highest priority and pursued as your deepest passion (Phil 3:8; compare Jer 9:23–24). When properly ordered, your academic studies can become an avenue by which you learn to abide in Christ and dwell in his presence. But this is not only your responsibility as a student. It must also be the posture of the faculty as well. Professors must teach with spiritual growth as the goal of their courses, regardless of their academic disciplines. Communicating information should never be equated with causing transformation, but teaching spiritual truth can be used to promote spiritual growth, and your seminary education should approach it that way.

In addition to being spiritual, *your seminary education should be biblical.* While most ministry institutions would affirm this in principle, a school's commitment to the Scriptures will be evidenced in its expressed doctrinal convictions regarding God's word and its corresponding role in their curriculum. Scripture teaches that the Bible is the verbal expression of God's divine revelation (2 Tim 3:16), written by human authors who were guided by the Holy Spirit (2 Pet 1:20–21). It is God's chosen means for salvation (1 Pet 1:23; 2 Tim 3:15) and sanctification (Jn 17:17; 2 Pet 2:2). In addition, his word is "living and powerful" and serves as his divine instrument for spiritual surgery (Heb 4:12) and his weapon for spiritual warfare (Eph 6:17). These truths all culminate in establishing the Bible as the inspired, inerrant, and infallible word of God that is sufficient as the sole and supreme authority for all of life.

As such, Scripture is the ultimate truth and the foundational standard for all knowledge. In seminary, the wide-ranging fields of study are joined together in the unified truth of Scripture. This means that every academic discipline must be informed by and infused with God's word. The content of every course should be measured against the plumbline of Scripture and taught according to its timeless and trustworthy nature. Beyond integrating Scripture into every field of study, seminary should also equip you to personally love, study, and apply God's word into every area of your own life. Along with developing your understanding of the Bible, seminary also equips you to perform essential aspects of gospel ministry that require the faithful handling of the Scriptures (2 Tim 2:15).

Another essential characteristic of your preparation is that *your seminary education should be theological.* This may be the most obvious attribute of academic training for ministry. However, many people wrongly assume that theological study consists of boring discussions about random doctrines and "ivory tower" musings that are divorced from everyday life and ministry. Sadly, some schools may approach it this way or, even worse, may distort a right understanding of God by constructing a theology according to their own conceptions of him. But sound theology that is developed according to the Scriptures and informed by historic orthodoxy can provide a confident assurance that bolsters your faith and deepens your affections for the Lord as you explore the unfathomable depths of the unsearchable riches of the knowledge of God (Rom 11:33).

Theological training also informs your understanding by helping you construct a biblical and theological worldview. Sound doctrine establishes moral guidelines that reflect God's character, offers hope in God's goodness and redemptive love, and gives meaning for your life in God's sovereign purposes. Beyond your own doctrinal development, studying theology will also translate into your ministry preparation. It will equip you to counsel God's people with understanding, prioritize essential doctrines that promote and preserve unity, and engage cultural issues with wisdom. While seminary preparation may include more than theological training, it certainly does not involve anything less.

A fourth characteristic for you to consider in your ministry preparation is that *your seminary education should be practical.* Every form of education runs the risk of becoming more theoretical than functional, and seminary is no different. For example, ministry principles discussed in the classroom do not always transfer into ministry practices in the church.

Similarly, you can easily read about church history and miss the contemporary relevance, or you can study theology and miss the practical implications. Often, while you are in seminary, the disconnect between the classroom and the church is a blind spot. But the goal should be to blend the "library" and the "laboratory" to allow your areas of study to inform your areas of service while your church ministry helps you process the class material.

Finally, *your seminary education should be missional.* As followers of Jesus, our marching orders are clear. After his death, burial, and resurrection, before returning to his heavenly throne, our Savior commanded us to make disciples of all nations (Matt 28:18–20). This command is not limited to those called to vocational ministry; it is true for all believers! But for those who have been called to ministry leadership, it does mean that you have a responsibility to train and prepare for the unique missional capacity in which God has called you to serve.

As a seminary seeks to provide this vocational ministry training, it must instill within you a heart to fulfill the Great Commission. This means that every degree, every course, and every assignment ought to contribute to your training to make disciples. Indeed, every classroom must be a Great Commission classroom!

We have gathered these essays for the purpose of helping you understand the big picture of your theological formation and ministry preparation. We want you to see how the pieces, or the various academic disciplines, fit together to form and shape you into the minister of the gospel that the Lord has called you to be.

The following chapters will walk through the foundational academic disciplines you will study in your seminary education. Each chapter will outline the field of study while also including and demonstrating the importance of spiritual formation, theological integration, ministry preparation, critical thinking, and communicating these truths to your audience.[4]

Read and Reflect: Ephesians 4:11–16

Prayer: *Our faithful God, who has called us to follow him and to proclaim the riches of his grace, help us to faithfully prepare for the task and work of ministry. Strengthen us and give us the heart and mind for the ministry task. Through Jesus Christ, our Lord. Amen.*

---

4. Southeastern Baptist Theological Seminary builds its curriculum and individual courses on five core competencies that are foundational to our degrees: Spiritual Formation, Biblical Exposition, Theological Integration, Ministry Preparation, and Critical Thinking and Communication. The discipline-specific chapters are outlined according to four of these since Biblical Exposition (the ability to properly and effectively interpret, apply, and communicate the Scriptures) undergirds each field of study and we have dedicated an entire chapter to it.

1

CONSIDER YOUR CALLING

R. Scott Pace

One of the most difficult concepts to learn in life is valuation. It clearly goes beyond simply learning how to read a price tag, but the additional aspects are not always obvious. Determining how to assign value and estimate worth, assessing the time and effort required to earn the money that something costs, and accounting for an ever-changing market can be a complicated process. At its most basic level, this is why you can tell a child that a toy that costs twenty dollars is too expensive, but he has no idea why that means that he cannot have it. You may have that amount of money in your pocket, but you know you can order the toy online for half the price and that the intense desire the child has for it at that moment is a misleading emotion that confuses an "extra" for an essential. He does not need it, despite his outbursts and attempts to convince you that he must have it.

Even though it is an easy problem to recognize with children and toys, the complexity of the issue is more evident in adults with the same struggles. Significant purchases, like the latest cellphone, a newer model car, designer clothes, or a house that is more than what they can sensibly afford, are often dictated by desires and emotions instead of what is wise or necessary. Now, before you mistake this book for a guide to personal finance and toss it aside, consider the greater and more important parallel concept that this reflects.

When it comes to our spiritual walk and, more specifically, God's call on our lives, we can have a tough time estimating the cost of pursuing God's will and evaluating the value of surrendering our lives to him. But this is a foundational aspect of the Christian life and an essential aspect of discipleship. Jesus reinforced this truth by posing it in the form of a valuation question: "For what does it profit a man if he gains the whole world and loses or forfeits himself?" (Luke 9:25).[1]

In the Gospel of Luke, one of the primary themes highlighted throughout the life and ministry of Jesus is costly discipleship. It is recognized early on with Jesus's calling of Peter, James, and John, where they ultimately "left everything and followed him" (Luke 5:11). The personal sacrifices involved in following Christ are repeatedly emphasized as our Savior challenges people to count the cost of surrendering to him (Luke 14:25–33; compare 9:23–25, 57–62; 18:18–30). His call to discipleship requires us to elevate our love for him above our earthly family (Luke 14:26), "renounce all" that we have (Luke 14:33), and refuse to look back (Luke 9:62). Jesus's call to follow him is challenging, convicting, and compelling! Although we may not be able to fully anticipate all that he will require of us, when we trust Christ for salvation, we are pledging our unconditional obedience and lifelong allegiance to him.

These passages were instrumental in discerning God's call on my life. Following my graduation from college, I began a

---

1. Scripture references from this chapter are from the English Standard Version.

successful career as an accountant and business manager. As I considered the depth of faith, the willingness to serve, and the abandoning of earthly pursuits that Jesus continually highlighted in his teaching, I was convicted that God was calling me to something more. I was living for Jesus, but I was working for myself. I was experiencing unprecedented spiritual growth in my life, serving in a variety of ministries in my local church, and seeing God work in ways that I never could have accomplished in my own strength or ability. Through the affirmation of others and prayerful consideration of my stewardship before God (Matt 25:14–30), I surrendered to God's call to vocational ministry.

Although not every disciple is called to serve Christ in this capacity, for some, the call to follow Christ involves a call to full-time ministry or missions. The unique nature of this calling requires seasons of preparation and specialized training. But before you launch into the equipping process, you must first "consider your calling" (1 Cor 1:26). Your calling requires you to count the cost of "building this tower" and to estimate the sacrifice of "engaging in this battle" (Luke 14:28–32). You must be aware of the sacrifice your calling will require but also the eternal value that makes every expense worth it. As you walk through this valuation process and answer his call, there are three important principles to be mindful of as you consider your calling.

YOUR CALL TO MINISTRY IS SPECIFIC

Over the years, the meaning of the term *calling* has shifted. Historically, saying someone was *called* was limited to a vocational missions or ministry capacity. More recently, to avoid an unhealthy division between leadership and laity and to emphasize all Christians' responsibility to serve God in the church and live on mission, we began to lighten that line of distinction for good and godly reasons. But sadly, we unintentionally went too far and erased it altogether so that now many believers never explore the possibility that they are called to serve the Lord in a vocational capacity.

However, it is important to recognize that the universal calling on all believers and the unique calling on individual disciples are not mutually exclusive; they do not present an either/or distinction but rather a both/and affirmation. Universally, Jesus invites us all to follow him with a call to salvation that includes a call to serve him and a call to surrender to his mission. In this sense, no matter what context we are living in or what career we are serving in, all believers are "called." We are all called to worship him, to walk with him, and to witness for him!

At the same time, *God calls you to serve in a specific capacity*. There is an individual aspect of God's calling that includes our vocation, and for some individuals this involves a setting apart for vocational ministry leadership. Throughout Scripture we see people designated for ministry roles that are specific to them. This includes the patriarchs of the faith like Noah (Gen 6), Abraham (Gen 12), Moses (Exod 3), David (1 Sam 16), Isaiah (Isa 6), and Jeremiah (Jer 1), along with faithful and instrumental servants like Deborah (Judg 4), Esther (Esth 4), and all the prophets, priests, and kings in the Old Testament. Similarly, in the New Testament the Lord chose twelve disciples for a specific purpose (Matt 10; John 15:16), and we see faithful servants like Stephen (Acts 7), Philip (Acts 8), the apostle Paul (Gal 1:15–16; 1 Cor 15:8), Lydia (Acts 16), Phoebe (Rom 16), and Epaphroditus (Phil 3) designated for unique ministry assignments.

The setting apart of certain individuals for vocational service to the Lord is frequently referred to in the New Testament as a *call* or *calling*. For example, Hebrews 5:4 refers to Aaron's priestly role as one that he was "called by God" to perform. Similarly, Abraham's obedience to follow God's plan is described as a response of faith "when he was called" (Heb 11:8). Paul references God's divine appointment for him to preach the gospel to the Gentiles as being "set apart" before he was born and one that was realized when God "called me by his grace" (Gal 1:15–16).

Paul also challenged followers of Christ to "consider your calling" (1 Cor 1:26). In using this phrase, he wanted believers to recognize that our salvation is not based on any merit, worth, skill, or any other "worldly standards" of qualification. But he also understands that our calling to salvation includes a specific role and task.[2] In fact, he uses the same term at the beginning of the first Corinthian letter in reference to God's individual purpose for his life: "Paul, called by the will of God to be an apostle of Christ Jesus" (1 Cor 1:1). So, as believers, when we speak about our calling, this term includes God's vocational intentions for our lives and his desire to leverage our work for the cause of Christ.

Today, God is still calling certain individuals to positions of vocational ministry leadership. But it is important to recognize that the specific nature of a call to ministry does not elevate certain individuals among God's people to an elite category or somehow signify that some people have more intrinsic value or spiritual significance than others. Ministry leaders are called "to equip the saints for the work of ministry" (Eph 4:11–12) as they serve God's flock and minister among them (1 Pet 5:2–4). Notice the value placed on the people and the shared work of

---

2. Roy E. Ciampa and Brian S. Rosner, *The First Letter to the Corinthians*, Pillar New Testament Commentary (Grand Rapids, MI: Eerdmans, 2010), 103–4.

ministry as they labor together for Christ. God's people are saints and sheep who belong to the chief shepherd. Therefore, we must understand that the distinction in calling is one of role, not worth. It is more a matter of assignment and responsibilities than ability or rank.

As you prayerfully consider your call to the ministry, it is essential for you to confirm and clarify your call. Charles Spurgeon, the renowned nineteenth-century preacher, famously described four primary factors involved in discerning your call to ministry.[3] First, you will experience an overwhelming passion that he describes as "an intense, all-absorbing desire for the work." This foundational aspect of your calling consumes your heart and will not allow you to be fulfilled pursuing another career capacity.[4] Second, Spurgeon notes that you will possess unique gifts that are essential for that work of ministry and are clearly recognizable. These gifts are confirmed by the third factor: God's blessing, which produces spiritual fruit through your service and affirms your usefulness as he honors your devotion. Finally, your calling is affirmed by others in the body of Christ as they observe your character, your gifts, and your effectiveness to be used by God.

Prayerfully wrestling through your calling is an important part of the discernment process that helps to anchor you for the storms of life and ministry. The confirmation season is vital to ensuring that you remain committed to your calling when you would otherwise be tempted to abandon it. Circumstantial hindsight can cause you to dismiss God's call as an emotional decision you made years earlier or one you felt pressure to

---

3. Charles Spurgeon, *Lectures to My Students: Complete and Unabridged* (Grand Rapids: Zondervan, 1980), 26–33.

4. Spurgeon, *Lectures to My Students*, 26.

embrace based on others' expectations. Your certainty is crucial, and you must avoid the temptation to short-circuit the confirmation process. Taking the time to work through the various personal, private, and public aspects of affirming your call is essential. Your ministry passion, spiritual gifts, personal fulfillment, and public affirmation will all serve to confirm the specific nature of your calling as you solidify your understanding of God's purpose for your life.

While your call to ministry is specific, this does not mean that you should define it too narrowly. Your calling is not defined by a particular gift, a certain role, or a ministry task. It is more of a ministry trajectory that focuses on direction instead of a destination. For instance, you can be called to serve as a student pastor, but this capacity does not restrict you from eventually serving as a senior pastor. If you are called to local church leadership, the pastoral nature of your calling is not necessarily confined to one type of position. Similarly, being "called to preach" may be an aspect or expression of your calling, but it cannot define it. When you delineate your calling too specifically, you can begin to limit the ways God desires to use you. Related to this, while your calling is for a lifetime, there may be seasonal aspects of it as well. Although you may be called to serve God vocationally on the mission field, you may one day serve as a missions pastor in a local church. This does not mean you are somehow abandoning your calling; it simply signifies a shift in your ministry capacity.

This type of transition highlights another aspect of your specific calling. In addition to serving him in a specific capacity, *God calls you to serve in a specific context.* This is an element that is often overlooked by those who are called to ministry. But God's sovereignty in your calling does not just relate to his gifts and overall plan for your life. It also includes how he weaves your abilities together with your individual experiences. This includes your family upbringing and your societal conditioning, your struggles and your successes, and your heart's passions and vocational aspirations (consider Paul's testimony in Gal 1:14–16; 1 Cor 15:9–10; and Phil 3:4–8). His providence in your life combines the timing of your conversion, spiritual growth, and the development of your ministry gifts into opportunities for service according to your calling.

As you faithfully serve in a vocational or volunteer capacity that corresponds with your giftedness, God will open doors according to his plan for your life. This means you do not have to stress or worry about when and where he will call you to serve. You do not have to manipulate circumstances or manufacture opportunities by attempting to impress others, leverage personal relationships, or position yourself for God to find you. He knows exactly where you are and how to get you where he desires you to be. This could mean that you must patiently endure seasons of growth in unfavorable circumstances that are preparing you for your next ministry assignment. But God's ability to network and navigate circumstances on your behalf is always trustworthy and often reveals his will in ways that make it undeniable.

YOUR CALL TO MINISTRY IS STRATEGIC

In addition to the specific nature of your calling, God has a strategic purpose in mind for you. From eternity past, the God who sovereignly "works all things according to the counsel of his will" and for "the praise of his glory" (Eph 1:11–12) has desired to use you as part of his master plan. At the end of his ministry, the apostle Paul was aware of the providential nature of God's plan for his life as he acknowledged, "The time for my departure has come" (2 Tim 4:6–8). His reflective thoughts came on the heels of his charge to Timothy, "Fulfill your ministry" (2 Tim 4:5). The specific ways God has gifted you and is preparing you for your calling confirms that your call to ministry is strategic.

It is important to recognize that the global nature of God's kingdom work can make it challenging to discern and pursue the strategic purpose of your calling. Because that work includes so many avenues of service, it can be difficult to know exactly what direction to choose or which decision to make. Ministry will require you to distinguish not only between "right" and "wrong," but between "good" and "best." As you learn to navigate these types of decisions, there are two guiding principles that will help you stay on track to fulfill the strategic purpose of your calling.

First, *your calling requires you to focus on the Master.* Fixing our eyes on Jesus is essential to running the race of the Christian life (Heb 12:1–2). But particularly in ministry, it is easy to become distracted. Distractions are sinful enticements that are related to our ministry responsibilities. For example, there is always a threatening danger that our leadership influence could devolve into condescending arrogance or for flattering words to seduce us into flirtatious misconduct; for public notoriety to transform into self-idolatry; or for generous gifts to lure us into presumptuous greed. Ministry is a minefield filled with the enemy's traps that explode with a simple misstep and shatter our lives with heart-piercing shrapnel. This is precisely why Paul charged Timothy as a "good soldier of Christ Jesus" and cautioned him against worldly distractions: "No soldier gets entangled in civilian pursuits, since his aim is to please the one who has enlisted him" (2 Tim 2:3–4). In ministry, your focus must be on honoring and obeying Jesus, your commanding officer. You cannot afford to be distracted by the cares of the world or allow your heart to be enticed by the seductive trappings of ministry leadership.

Sometimes it is not the sinful temptations that distract us; it is the subtle temptations that can divert our attention from focusing on our Master. In ministry, it is easy to mistake busyness for faithfulness and diligence for devotion. Like Jesus's industrious friend Martha, we can become "distracted with much serving." We can be so consumed with working for the Lord that we fail to worship him. But, like her sister Mary, we must prioritize intimacy with Christ, remembering that only "one thing is necessary." We cannot exchange "the good portion" of loving and listening to Jesus for ministry chores that cause us to be "anxious and troubled about many things" (Luke 10:38–42). In ministry, busyness is a greater danger than idleness. Following Christ and serving others is a "work of faith and labor of love," but remember that your work and labor should always be produced by your sincere faith and fervent love (1 Thess 1:3). These can only be cultivated through intimate fellowship and meaningful time with your Savior.

Focusing on the Master includes avoiding sinful, subtle distractions, but it also involves a devotion and loyalty that knows and listens to the voice of the Good Shepherd (John 10:3–4). In life and ministry, there will be competing voices that attempt to persuade you to follow conventional wisdom. These voices, which can include our own selfish desires or well-intending loved ones, can mislead us with the best of intentions. With genuine concern, those who care about us can gently appeal to our own desires to settle for convenience and comfort rather than pursue obedience and sacrifice. The decisions your Savior calls you to make will not always be popular, and your friends and family will not always understand. But your ultimate allegiance to Christ must result in your unqualified obedience to

Christ. If you find yourself seeking the approval of others, you are no longer honoring and following the Master (Gal 1:10).

This leads us to the second guiding principle necessary to accomplish the strategic purpose of your calling. Not only are you called to focus on the Master, *but your calling also requires you to fulfill his mission.* We have seen how Scripture describes our service to Christ as a soldier obeying his commanding officer (2 Tim 2:3–4). But the most important aspect of this military imagery is the implication of a kingdom mission for which we have been enlisted. Like any battle regime, each soldier in God's armed forces has an assignment that is essential to fulfilling the mission. This is the primary reason your calling is strategic. You are an ambassador of the King! You have been charged with the assignment to speak on his behalf, sharing the good news of salvation that is available through Jesus (2 Cor 5:18–20).

When it comes to fulfilling his mission, the strategic aspect for God's calling is best understood by considering your context. Think about this: God's will for your life involves a *particular* ministry in a *specific* community with *certain* individuals at a *chosen* time in history. All these elements of your life and ministry combine into a unique opportunity and responsibility that God has given *you*! This reality has significant implications. It means that you cannot dismiss or minimize the importance of any of these providential elements in your ministry. It means you must carefully discern your ministry opportunities and not just accept any position offered. It means that you cannot simply abandon your ministry outpost when difficulties or troubles arise. It also means that there is no place for comparison to others' ministries. You cannot be disgruntled because your ministry is not as ideal as you think someone else's is, and you cannot be disappointed because you feel like you deserve better. You also cannot be prideful over the blessings of your ministry and relish in the lack of misfortune that others may be experiencing in theirs. God providentially places you in your ministry and orchestrates your circumstances to work in your life and to accomplish his will (Rom 8:28; Gen 50:20).

The humbling and exciting reality of God's call on your life is the role he calls you to play in his kingdom. It is amazing! But if we focus too narrowly on our ministry assignment, we can lose sight of the broader work of God's redemptive plan and begin to have an unhealthy balance. When we do, our hearts can become prideful, our prayers can become selfish, and our plans can become frustrated. However, when we concentrate on the wider view of his eternal kingdom, we can keep our personal call and responsibility in its proper perspective. To maintain a healthy and balanced understanding of the strategic nature of our calling, we must simply focus on following the Master and fulfilling his mission!

YOUR CALL TO MINISTRY IS SIGNIFICANT

Considering your calling can provoke a wide range of emotions. The spiritual gravity of your calling should humble you. The potential impact of your calling can motivate you. The unknown future of your calling can terrify you. And the required sacrifices of your calling can overwhelm you. The magnitude and multitude of these various responses, along with a host of other feelings it can elicit, all demonstrate the significance of your calling. Being set apart for ministry leadership is not something to be taken lightly!

At the same time, the significance of your calling is not primarily determined by the impact it has on you. Its ultimate significance is measured in the difference it makes for Christ. The magnitude of this reality is even more daunting than the personal emotions our calling can provoke. God will use your service for Christ to work in the lives of others, and as a result, your ministry responsibilities will elevate your accountability to him (Jas 3:1). Let that sink in for a moment.

The significance of this reality even caused the apostle Paul to lament the weight of spiritual responsibility he felt for the people he was called to serve. For the lost, he anguished over their spiritual condition with passion and prayers for them to be saved (Rom 9:1–3; 10:1). And concerning God's church, he acknowledged that the spiritual burden he felt exceeded any circumstantial difficulty or suffering that his ministry required (2 Cor 11:23–28). But God showed Paul that his grace was sufficient, and he offers us the same reassurance (2 Cor 12:9–10). As you embrace the gravity of your calling and the burden you have for the people God has called you to serve, you can do so with two important assurances in mind.

First, you can pursue your calling with the assurance that *God equips people for leadership roles.* Most job opportunities list required levels of training and experience that are necessary for the position. In service to the Lord, none of us has the necessary qualifications that would certify us for his work. Yet, in Christ, God qualifies us to share in his eternal enterprise (Col 1:12). This humbling reality should promote the same sincere disposition that Paul expressed as he considered the impact of his ministry and his unworthiness to be used by God: "Who is sufficient for these things?" (2 Cor 2:16). The truth is none of us are worthy. Yet, like Paul, we have been called and commissioned to serve the Lord (2 Tim 1:9–11).

Because of Christ's work on our behalf, we are qualified to work on his behalf. Christ redeems us so that we might be his people who are "zealous for good works" (Titus 2:14). Christ recreates us so that we can perform the good works he prepared for us (Eph 2:10). And Christ reconciles us so that we can fulfill our calling as ambassadors in leading others to faith in him (2 Cor 5:18–20). As a result, whatever inadequacies, insufficiencies, and insecurities you may feel concerning your calling can all be overcome because your qualifications are based on his merit, not your own. Your identity in Christ qualifies you for the gospel service God employs you to do (1 Pet 2:9).

But the confidence we have that God equips us for ministry leadership is not only based on identity in Christ, it is also grounded in our sufficiency in him. The abilities, talents, skills, and passions that you have are gifts from God that are specific for you and are essential elements of calling. And through Christ, God assures us that he will "equip [us] with everything good that [we] may do his will" (Heb 13:21; compare 2 Pet 1:3). In other words, God's will for your life will not require something from you that he will not provide for. And as you work hard to faithfully develop and sharpen his tools in your life, "God is able to make *all* grace abound to you, so that having *all sufficiency* in *all things* at *all times*, you may abound in *every* good work" (2 Cor 9:8, emphasis added). The highlighted superlatives in this verse should translate as exclamation points of God's reassurances for you. While the everyday realities of life in ministry will challenge and attempt to undermine these timeless truths and cause you to question God's faithfulness, you can trust that God equips those he calls to ministry leadership.

In addition to knowing that God equips people for leadership roles, you can also confidently pursue your calling knowing that *he employs people in leadership roles.* Like every vocation, God's employment involves both your qualifications and your compensation. In addition to your qualifications in Christ, God also provides scriptural assurance of the vocational nature of your calling to ministry. For example, in the

Old Testament, the Lord compensates the Levites and their families for their service through designated portions and provisions (Num 18:21; compare 1 Cor 9:13). Likewise, in the New Testament, the church is instructed to honor ministry leaders with financial support (1 Tim 5:17–18; 1 Cor 9:6–12). Those who are called to devote themselves to a lifetime of gospel ministry are supported in their service (1 Cor 9:14).

To earn a living by serving the Lord and his people is a privilege that should cause humility and ought never be taken for granted. The salary and support received is a gracious provision from God. The Scripture cautions to guard the heart from being motivated by a desire for financial gain (1 Tim 6:6–10; compare 1 Pet 5:2; 1 Tim 3:3; Titus 1:7). While vocationally employed, we are not career professionals who simply pull a paycheck for rendering service in a ministry context. We are not looking to advance up the positional ladder of status, and we are not working to accumulate material wealth. As those who are called by God, we must simply desire to be faithful servants who trust the Lord to provide for our families. According to his riches in Christ, he assures us that he will (Phil 4:19).

All these aspects of God's provisions mean that you are a steward. God has entrusted you with gifts, resources, and opportunities to leverage for his kingdom and his mission. The impact your life can have for the cause of Christ is significant, and he will equip you with everything you need to fulfill his calling on your life!

CONCLUSION

As you pursue God's will, it is critical to "consider your calling." The Lord sets apart individuals for certain roles in his redemptive plan. His call involves a specific capacity according to your spiritual gifts and passions. He incorporates everything from background to present circumstances to compose a perfect plan. With these things in mind, he also calls you to a context that weds personal experience with service opportunities. Your call to the ministry is specific. It is custom made with a you-shaped hole and a God-sized opportunity.

Your call to the ministry is also strategic. God's mission to engage a lost world with the gospel and his intention to use you makes you a target for the enemy. To avoid the enticing temptations and hindering distractions that come with ministry, you must keep your focus on the Master. Fixing your eyes on Jesus will allow you to fulfill his mission. His strategic calling positions you to serve him in a certain place, with a chosen people, for a particular season that he has providentially prepared for you. And that is what he wants to prepare you for!

In addition to being specific and strategic, your call to the ministry is also significant. But this is not based on your significance, and your calling does not make you significant. Your call to ministry is significant because of the magnitude of God's kindness in Christ to qualify undeserving sinners like us to be used for his glory (1 Tim 1:12–17) and because of his exceedingly great power to accomplish unimaginable things through inadequate and imperfect people like you and me (Eph 3:20–21).

Understanding the specific, strategic, and significant nature of your calling elevates your responsibility to leverage your life for the gospel. As a result, the importance of preparation to fulfill your calling cannot be overstated. It deserves and demands your careful consideration because you are called to grow (2 Pet 3:18)! Our prayer is that this book will be a helpful resource for your journey in pursuing God's call on your life. We hope that it will serve as an encouraging guide as you explore the value and role of seminary education for your ministry preparation. So, in the words of the apostle Paul, we challenge you to "consider your calling" (1 Cor 1:26).

Read and Reflect: 1 Timothy 3:1–16

Prayer: *Father, we make many plans, but you establish our steps. Grant by your grace that we faithfully carry out the ministry you have set before us, both today and for the span of our lives. Through Jesus Christ, our Lord. Amen.*

2

CHRISTIAN THEOLOGY FOR MINISTRY PREPARATION

Daniel L. Akin and Jonathan D. Six

"I want the Bible, but you can keep your theology." When a church member shared this remark with me (Jonathan), I was a young minister and had no idea how to respond. Didn't theology come from the text of Scripture? For the first time in my young faith, I had to ask where my theology came from. I knew that Christian theology was essential for the minister of the gospel. I also knew that a minister who seeks to serve the church must have a solid handle on the great doctrines of the Bible. What was missing in this conversation with my concerned parishioner? In short, this brother assumed the truth of the Bible but also believed that theology was an individual abstraction of what the Bible teaches. This notion could not be further from the truth. Instead, the truths of the Bible are ultimate and objective. Theology seeks to know God, not through simple observation but through the study of God's divine self-revelation. Through this study, God's divine nature, his created world, and the purpose of his redemptive work are known. We see and know God and how he works within his world through theology.

The word *theology* means "the study of God," and terms such as *doctrine* emphasize the great teachings of the Christian faith. The comprehensive analysis of the Bible produces propositional truths about God. Through divine revelation, God has disclosed his perfect character and ultimate *telos* for his creation. As some theologians argue, "Christian theology is (the) disciplined reflection of God's self-revelation."[1] Throughout the text of Scripture, various doctrines form a holistic Christian theology, which helps one to contend for the faith once for all delivered to the saints (Jude 3).[2]

CHRISTIAN THEOLOGY AND THE FORMATION OF DOCTRINE

Christian theology is an integrated discipline that draws upon other studies that help the theologian to reflect and articulate a biblically faithful theology. For example, Christian theology depends upon the analysis or interpretation of the Scripture to formulate doctrinal conclusions. Further, philosophy helps the theologian situate the Christian faith within the larger framework of ontology and epistemology. The theologian draws from the philosophical well in considering the existence of God, the nature of reality, and the exploration of truth, among other things. Other disciplines, such as biblical theology and historical theology, help to give insights into the forming of doctrine from the biblical text and the practice of the church throughout history.

---

1. Bruce R. Ashford and Keith Whitfield, "Theological Method: An Introduction to the Task of Theology," in *A Theology for the Church*, edited by Daniel L. Akin, rev. ed. (Nashville: B&H Academic, 2014), 3.

2. Scripture references in this chapter refer to the Christian Standard Bible.

Christian theology includes various doctrines ranging from the doctrine of revelation to eschatology. Each of these doctrines is studied independently, yet they are interdependent. For example, how one understands the nature of Scripture will ultimately shape one's doctrine of sin. Likewise, how one understands the doctrine of sin will inform one's doctrine of salvation. Thus, Christian theology integrates the various doctrines that arise from the text of Scripture.

Many Christian theology texts begin with the doctrine of revelation, which typically includes discussion on theological method, divine revelation, and natural revelation. A theological method is generally defined as *how* one moves from the Bible to doctrine, or teaching about who God is. Discussions of divine revelation center on the nature of Scripture as an inspired revelation from God. Included here is the character of Scripture, which is without error and not lacking in any way. Further, the authority and sufficiency of Scripture are also explored. Natural revelation analyzes how nature reveals God's divine power and attributes from within the created order, and it is universal for all people to observe. These doctrines collectively explain how God makes himself known.

Some theology texts begin with the doctrine of God, which explores God's existence, being, trinitarian nature, divine attributes, and work of creation and providence. The doctrine of God is often referred to as "theology proper." From beginning to end, the Bible attests to, assumes, and confirms God's existence and work among his creation. Theology proper forms into an integrated whole the Bible's teaching about God's being, nature, and work within creation.

Another important doctrine is the doctrine of humanity. This doctrine helps explain what it means to be a human created in God's image and explores humanity's end or purpose.

Often referred to as biblical anthropology, a biblical view of humanity is vital to understanding complex ethical issues such as abortion, sexuality, and end-of-life issues.

Related to the doctrine of humanity is the doctrine of human sinfulness. This doctrine explores the origin of sin and how sin impacts humanity individually and corporately. Definitions of sin and sinfulness will often shape one's definition of salvation. If our understanding of human sinfulness is not robust, we will see no need for a robust gospel of redemption.

Fundamental to Christian theology is the doctrine of Christ. Most theologians divide the doctrine of Christ into two parts. First is the person of Christ, which explores the divine and human natures of Jesus, his virgin birth, holiness, and power. Second is the work of Christ, which explores Jesus's work on the cross, resurrection, ascension, and return. Together, these form the christological foundation of the Christian faith.

The doctrine of the Holy Spirit is essential to the trinitarian nature of the Godhead. Explorations of the nature and person of the Holy Spirit are crucial to determining the work of the Holy Spirit within the Christian faith. This doctrine is often known as pneumatology, and it articulates the biblical teaching of the Holy Spirit and provides a theological framework for the Spirit's work within the church.

The doctrine of salvation, often known as soteriology, explains the components and work of salvation for the individual and the final restoration of all things. Topics addressed in soteriology are issues such as the *ordo salutis* (the order of salvation); the conditions of salvation—conversion, repentance, and regeneration; the components of salvation—justification, sanctification, and glorification; and the final state of salvation, the restoration of all things. These collectively form the doctrine of salvation.

How do those who are redeemed gather together to worship the Lord? The church is the assembly of God's people in both a local and universal sense. The Bible spells out the specifics of who are members of the church. The Bible refers to the church as a body (Rom 12:4–5, 1 Cor 12:27). The Bible speaks of the church as a flock that the elders shepherd (Acts 20:28). Matthew and Paul discuss the process of discipline and excommunication (Matt 18:15–17; 1 Cor 5:12–13). The point here is that the Bible describes the church as the redeemed of God, those born again and walking in repentance and faith.

Ecclesiology also gives direction for the governance and leadership of the church. Disagreements among evangelical denominations on the leadership structure and authority of the church often center on how to interpret the offices of pastor, elder, and overseer. Most Baptists affirm congregational church governance, with the leadership of the church entrusted to the office of the pastor/elder. In 2023 the Southern Baptist Convention voted to explicitly state in the *Baptist Faith and Message* that the office of pastor/elder/overseer is a singular office. The change in this confession is an example of how the study of theology informs and shapes church practice.

Eschatology, or the doctrine of last things, provides the doctrinal basis for Jesus's second advent and the process whereby God will restore his good creation to its intended purpose. While there are significant differences among eschatological positions, all views include Christ's physical return to earth and the establishment of the eternal kingdom. Eschatology in many ways functions as a theological lens that shapes biblical interpretation, definitions of the church, God's relationship to Israel, and the establishment of God's kingdom economy.

There are practical implications of eschatology for both ethics and global missions. For example, if our notion of eschatology is that God's kingdom is only in the future, the impetus for cultural engagement will be lacking. Conversely, if we believe that our work within the culture somehow ushers in God's kingdom reign, we will be active in our ethical and cultural engagement. Likewise, if we believe the primary thrust of the Christian faith is inaugurating God's kingdom, the primary focus of missions will likely be cultural. Further, if we believe that God will restore Israel during a time of tribulation, there might be theological objections to missions among the Jews. Eschatology has significant practical implications.

CHRISTIAN THEOLOGY APPLIED

Theology is the driving force behind Christian missions, the formation of the church, and beliefs about salvation and spiritual health. Christian theology is a gained knowledge rooted in revelation that results in worship and service to God. In short, the study of Christian theology is not about acquiring knowledge *per se* but rather the cultivation of wisdom, worship, and obedience. Done rightly, the study of God produces outcomes—faith, obedience, worship, and Great Commission fervor.

CHRISTIAN THEOLOGY AND THE PRESERVATION OF BIBLICAL ORTHODOXY

Studying Christian theology for ministry preparation is vital for the health and preservation of the church's doctrine. It is often the case that practice drives belief rather than belief driving practice. The study of Christian theology provides the guardrails for pursuing and exercising ministry within the church context. Theology should be rightly oriented and ought to drive the church to a more profound sense of God's mission to redeem and result in a greater understanding of worship. If the starting place is pragmatic and not an application of theology, the missional thrust is lost by the desire for pragmatic outcomes.

Christian theology helps to preserve the faith once for all delivered to the saints (Jude 3). The great church councils and historic confessions provide a snapshot of how a deep commitment to studying theology preserves biblical orthodoxy. When one pursues Christian theology to reflect on God and his word, and apply it to his world, a beautiful vision of orthodoxy emerges and pushes the theologian into the mission of God. The faith endures because of a deep commitment to biblical faithfulness and theological accuracy.

CHRISTIAN THEOLOGY AND MISSION

I (Daniel) have often said that the greatest Christian missionary was the greatest Christian theologian. The apostle Paul models for us that when theology is rightly done, it leads to gospel ministry and mission. One looks no further than the apostle Paul's missional methodology. Whether he is in the synagogues or the Areopagus, he reasons from the Scripture to demonstrate who God is and that he (God) is redeeming through Christ's work on the cross and resurrection. These realities drive Paul deeper into ministry and mission. Paul does not seek out a fad or some complex strategy for ministry. Instead he simply teaches the truths of Scripture and calls his hearers to repentance and faith. Not only does the faith spread, but the rich doctrines of the church spread through the apostle's teachings. The Great Commission has this in view when Jesus calls his followers to make disciples, baptize them, and teach them all the Lord's commands. This certainly has theological implications. The call of the Great Commission is not merely for the sake of conversions but rather a call to make disciples who deeply understand the Christian faith. Without teaching the depths of theological truth, the fulfillment of the Great Commission is in question.

As gospel ministers, we must be careful what we multiply (Jas 3:1). Those who teach, counsel, or lead must have a firm grasp of Christian theology to ensure that what they pass along to others is orthodox. Very few heretics genuinely sought heresy, but rather they did not understand orthodoxy's limits. Therefore, in their ignorance, they were passing along a biblically anemic Christian faith.

CHRISTIAN THEOLOGY AND THE BUILDING UP OF YOUR FAITH

I (Jonathan) remember being told that seminary would cause you to question every teaching of the Bible and the Bible itself. While there might be a time in the history of some evangelical seminaries in which that was true, my prayer is that it is no longer the case. Theology taught rightly does not cause you to give up your theological convictions but rather buttresses your faith. Evangelical Christian theology affirms the veracity of Scripture, the transcendent yet knowable God, the trinitarian nature of the Godhead, the virgin birth of the Son, the penal substitutionary atonement of Jesus, his resurrection, and his promised return to gather his church and fully establish his kingdom.

These doctrines are not mere abstractions but the backbone of the Christian faith. When these doctrines are reflected upon, confessed, and allowed to shape one's life, faith is built up. Moreover, these theological truths have significant practical implications. The reality of who God is and his redemptive purpose has substantial ethical and missional implications. Recognizing that God loved us enough to send his Son to be an atoning sacrifice, paying the penalty due us, is a massive encouragement to the soul.

CHRISTIAN THEOLOGY AND FAITHFUL OBEDIENCE

"The fear of the Lord is the beginning of wisdom" (Prov 9:10). Theology drives one to know God, but it also drives one know God's world and live faithfully in it. As Proverbs continues, "Knowledge of the Holy One is understanding" (Prov 9:10). The pattern of Moses was to remind his reader of Yahweh and then call his people to obedience (Exod 20:2). The knowledge of God calls one to faithfully obey God's divine law and moral standards. Christian ethics, then, is produced from Christian theology. As your knowledge of God grows, so should your worship and obedience to the Lord. Theology driving obedience is the apostle Paul's model in Romans as well. In chapter 6, Paul provides ten indicatives, theological statements of fact, before he calls for action. Paul is rooting obedience to God in theological fact, not mere obligation. As the vision of God grows, our understanding of his holiness grows, the gospel of God expands, and our own obedience also grows.

Practically speaking, theology conforms us to God's vision of himself. Our obedience is therefore conformed to the theological realities of God's salvation in Christ, his restoration of all things, and the moral standards spelled out in the Bible. Thus, all of life is submitted to God's lordship. Our views of life, marriage, sexuality, money, and love are all rooted deeply in theological truth. In teaching theological truth, the church teaches profound truths that help our members walk faithfully in obedience.

CONCLUSION

It should not come as a surprise that seminary professors believe that teaching theology is essential for ministry preparation. In this short essay, we sought to bring a deeper understanding of the centrality of knowing Christian theology and having it shape both the student and those whom they serve. First, we have argued that Christian theology is essential for spiritual formation. If the chief end of man is to glorify God and enjoy him forever,[3] then knowing God is essential. Theological inquiry and the study of the word of God is how we know God. The point is that theology drives spiritual formation. Without theology there is no true spiritual growth. There is also a warning here. The pursuit of theology without spiritual growth is equally harmful. Theological analysis and the formation of doctrine ought to drive one to worship, not isolation and arrogance.

Second, there is a reciprocal relationship between theology and Bible exposition. Good theological inquiry is based on sound commitments to the nature of Scripture, a faithful hermeneutic, and the authority of the Bible for theological formation. Likewise, expositors are also dependent upon theologians to draw out and connect the important doctrinal themes that arise from faithfully teaching the Bible.

Third, this chapter demonstrates that theology is not an end in itself but is integrated into other disciplines. While Christian theology depends upon biblical scholars and philosophers, so too do they depend upon theologians. Furthermore, almost every discipline uses theology. The ethicist applies theological truth to live in obedience to the Lord. The expositor is careful to point out the rich theological truths of the word of God. The counselor informs and shapes their counseling with deep theological truths. The evangelist and missiologist are motivated by God's redemptive work within the world.

Fourth, studying theology helps the student to think critically and communicate clearly. As the old adage goes, everyone

3. See the *Westminster Shorter Catechism*.

is a theologian; the question is whether you are a good one. Students must learn to critically analyze the biblical text and theological texts to determine their alignment. Those who teach must be able to spot heresy and give warnings of wolves in sheep's clothing (Matt 7:15). But the student, too, must be careful. Words have meaning, and careful explanation and theological clarity are of the utmost importance. Studying theology forces the student to critically analyze doctrine and clearly communicate doctrine in a true and helpful way.

Finally, it is essential to apply theology. Theology is not an end in itself but is for the purpose of making disciples and teaching them to obey all of the Lord's commands (Matt 28:20). Theology is for ministry preparation. Remember the story we started with about the brother who was not interested in learning theology? His only interaction with theology was divisive and harmful to his faith, but theology should encourage and equip the saints for the work of ministry. This brother had missed out on rich theological truths that would drive him deeper in love with God. Our prayer is that your study of Christian theology produces an incredibly rich love for the Lord and desire to invite others into this knowledge of the Holy One.

Read and Reflect: Romans 6:1–14

Prayer: *Incomprehensible God, who has nevertheless made himself known to us in your Son, Christ Jesus, may we know you more and more each day, be heralds of your revelation to those who do not yet know you, and long for the day when we see you face to face. Through Jesus Christ, our Lord. Amen.*

3

BIBLICAL STUDIES FOR MINISTRY PREPARATION

Charles L. Quarles

The study of the Holy Scriptures must form the core of any responsible training that seeks to prepare men and women for effective and faithful Christian ministry. No other book or books can rival the Bible in importance for evangelizing the lost, discipling believers, establishing churches, edifying the saints, comforting the grieving, strengthening the weak, calming the anxious, conquering evil, or glorifying our crucified and resurrected Savior. Thus, the Bible is indisputably the most important textbook for ministry preparation.

The Bible is far more than a mere textbook, and to treat it as any other textbook would be a despicable act of sacrilege. We should cherish this book as a treasure, for, as our Baptist confession exclaims, the Bible is a "perfect treasure of divine instruction." Other books in our curriculum were written by fallible human beings, but this book "is totally true and trustworthy" since it has "God for its author, salvation for its end, and truth without any mixture of error for its matter" (*Baptist Faith and Message* I).

ACCURATE BIBLICAL INTERPRETATION FOR MINISTRY

Every believer should strive to understand the Bible because these "sacred Scriptures . . . are able to give you wisdom for salvation through faith in Christ Jesus" (2 Tim 3:15).[1] Everyone who desires to increase in Christlikeness and serve God effectively should study the Bible, since "all Scripture is inspired by God and is profitable for teaching, for rebuking, for correcting, for training in righteousness, so that the man of God may be complete, equipped for every good work" (2 Tim 3:16–17). Accurately interpreting the Bible should be among the highest priorities of any who are tasked with explaining the Scriptures, whether they do so in the context of one-on-one evangelism, small group discipleship, from the lectern in a classroom, or from the pulpit of a church.

The apostle Paul charged Timothy in 2 Timothy 2:15: "Be diligent to present yourself to God as one approved, a worker who doesn't need to be ashamed, correctly teaching the word of truth." The imperative that Paul uses refers to giving yourself fully to a task, making your best effort, being dedicated to the work. Paul illustrates this diligence with a vivid illustration. He says that Timothy is to "correctly teach" the word of truth. The word translated "correctly teach" is *orthotomeō*, which means "to cut straight." Since the context uses agricultural imagery to portray Timothy's role (2 Tim 2:6) and refers to Timothy as a "worker" (a term most frequently used of agricultural laborers), Paul probably has the picture of a farmhand cutting a straight furrow in mind. A diligent farmhand in Paul's time would drive a stake at two adjacent corners of his field, stretch a string between those two stakes, and use that string as a guide for

1. All Scripture references come from the Christian Standard Bible, unless otherwise noted.

the plow so that he could meticulously plow the furrow as straight as possible. The worker knew that at the end of the day, the master of the estate would inspect his work, and he wanted those beautiful, neat, perfectly aligned rows to show the master that he had taken great pains to do his absolute best work. The straight furrow demonstrated that he approached his task with a commitment to accuracy and precision.[2] In the same way, Paul says that we who proclaim the word are spiritual farmhands who should be meticulous in our effort to plow a straight furrow with the word of truth. We dare not approach the task of interpreting God's word casually or flippantly. We strive for accuracy and precision in our exposition of Scripture. We are deeply concerned to handle God's word well.

Paul reminds us that the Master will inspect the field that we have plowed. He will examine the straightness of the furrows. He will judge whether we have accurately handled his word. The preacher or teacher who has correctly taught the word will not need to be ashamed. The shame that Paul is describing here is clearly a far deeper shame than mere public embarrassment, as frightening as that is. The word *present* is a legal term that speaks of presenting yourself to a judge for a verdict. Thus, Paul is describing the shame that the preacher or teacher will know on judgment day when he stands before God to give an account for what he has preached and taught and discovers that he has warped and perverted the word of God. But Paul emphasizes here that the preacher and teacher will be judged based on the accuracy of the messages we have preached. If we have preached the truth accurately, we will be approved and will stand before God unashamed. If we have preached error, we will stand before God disapproved and in shame.[3] We will

2. Our word *precise* uses a root meaning "to cut" to communicate accuracy.

3. See James 3:1.

not be judged by how clever our sermons are. We will not be judged by the number of people who come to hear us preach or teach. We will not be judged according to the numbers who repent and believe in response to our preaching. We will be judged by the accuracy of the message as an expression of the revealed truth of God. When God examines our proclamation of the word, he will not be impressed by our clever alliteration, by our catchy and trendy phrases, by our charismatic personalities, by our moving illustrations. Only the one who makes every effort to accurately expound the word will hear the words, "Well done, good and faithful servant."

KNOWLEDGE OF BIBLICAL LANGUAGES FOR MINISTRY

We can faithfully proclaim the gospel of salvation from any good translation of the Bible. This is due to the perspicuity of Scripture. Because of this essential clarity of the Bible, the *Second London Baptist Confession* of 1689 correctly states that "those things which are necessary to be known, believed and observed for salvation, are so clearly propounded and opened in some place of scripture or other, that not only the learned, but the unlearned, in a due use of ordinary means, may attain to a sufficient understanding of them" (I.7). The Confession adds that the Scriptures should be translated into the language of every nation so that those who do not know Hebrew and Greek "may worship him in an acceptable manner, and through patience and comfort of the scriptures may have hope" (I.8). Yet the Confession adds that since the Hebrew OT and Greek NT were directly inspired by God, "in all controversies of religion, the church is to finally appeal to them" (I.8). The Bible *in the original languages* is the final authority because all translations are, by necessity, human interpretations. Article 10 of the

Chicago Statement on Biblical Inerrancy recognizes this same distinction when it states: "Inspiration, strictly speaking, applies only to the autographic text," that is, the original texts of the Hebrew Old Testament and Greek New Testament. It adds, "Copies and translations of Scripture are the Word of God to the extent that they faithfully represent the original."

How faithfully do our translations represent the original text? Very well, and our finest translations are steadily improving. However, any translation is by necessity an interpretation, and the interpretations of even the best translators differ. This is why we can compare even the best translations and find that the translations of a specific verse not only differ in wording but also differ in meaning. In those cases in which the translations differ in meaning, at least one has misunderstood the original text. Every translator must make important decisions about the meaning of the original text in his effort to communicate its meaning to readers in other languages. No translator can do so perfectly. I am not aware of any English translation of the Bible that claims to be a perfect translation. Although some Christians have argued that the King James Version of 1611 is perfect, the translators of the version explicitly denied this. They argued that their translation should be respected and accepted due to its general character and despite its minor faults. In the section, "An Answer to the Imputations of Our Adversaries," the translators argued that a man could be considered handsome even though he had flaws such as warts on his hand, freckles on his face, and scars on his body. They concluded,

> No cause therefore why the word translated should be denied to be the word, or forbidden to be current, notwithstanding that some imperfections and blemishes

> may be noted in the setting forth of it. For whatever was perfect under the sun, where apostles or apostolic men—that is, men endued with an extraordinary measure of God's Spirit, and privileged with the privilege of infallibility—had not their hand?

The translators were acknowledging that they were not apostles or companions of the apostles (such as Luke, Mark, and the brothers of the Lord) and thus were neither inspired nor infallible. Consequently, their translation, despite their best efforts, had imperfections and blemishes. Since translations are not directly inspired by God like the original text of Scripture was, and since no translation can perfectly and completely express what God revealed in his word, the ability to read and study the Scriptures in the original languages is immensely valuable, especially for those who teach and preach the Scriptures.

Those who wish to teach only the obvious truths of Scripture and to summarize larger portions of the biblical text in their lessons or sermons can usually do so accurately by comparing a few faithful translations of the Bible. Those who want to teach or preach the details of Scripture, focusing on the meaning of single words, specific phrases, and grammatical constructions, should seek to learn biblical languages to ensure that they interpret Scripture accurately. Mastery of biblical languages will prevent exegesis from devolving into eisegesis. Even basic familiarity with biblical languages will grant the interpreter access to the most helpful and insightful resources for biblical study. I have encountered many detractors over the years who have adamantly argued that learning Hebrew and Greek is a waste of time. I have observed that they all share a common trait. They do not know Hebrew and Greek well! I trust that these advisors dearly love the word of God. I must assume that if they knew these languages well and had seen their significant importance for biblical interpretation, they would implore you to seize any opportunity that you may have to learn the languages of Scripture.

THE RELEVANCE OF BIBLICAL LANGUAGE STUDY FOR CHRISTIAN THEOLOGY AND ETHICS

Let me now offer a few examples of the relevance of knowledge of biblical languages for the correct interpretation of Scripture. I will present examples in which knowledge of biblical languages confirms the essential doctrine of the deity of Jesus Christ, enriches our understanding of biblical theology, guards the church from aberrant practices, and offers moral guidance regarding important trends in our culture.

THE DEITY OF JESUS

Colossians 1:15–20 contains a great hymn that exalts and glorifies Jesus. However, traditional English translations of one important phrase unintentionally prompt a grave misunderstanding of Jesus's identity. The King James Version translates the final phrase of verse 15 as "the firstborn of every creature." The English Standard Version and New American Standard Bible prefer the translation "the firstborn of all creation." Unfortunately, modern English readers encountering this expression for the first time usually assume that "of" means "who is a part of." However, no preposition appears in the Greek text of this phrase. "All creation" is in the genitive case, and this case can express dozens of different relationships between the head noun "firstborn" and the genitive modifier "creation." The ordinary English reader assumes the meaning of the partitive genitive ("the firstborn who is a part of all creation").

This would imply that Jesus is a created being, not the eternal Creator, incarnate Deity. This was the view of the ancient heretic Arius, whose diminished view of Jesus was soundly and rightly condemned by the early church in multiple councils and creeds. Although the Greek genitive may mean "is a part of" in some other contexts, it clearly does not here. The title "firstborn" expresses supreme authority drawn from the description of the king in Psalm 89:27: "I will also make him my firstborn, greatest of the kings of the earth." After a title of authority, the genitive noun ordinarily identifies the realm over which a figure rules, his royal domain. Examples include "the king of Israel" (Israel is the realm of the king), "the Lord of the earth" (the Lord rules over the earth), or "the master of the house" (the master has authority over the house). Paul is not claiming that Christ belongs to creation and is thus a created being. He is describing Christ as the greatest king and all creation as his realm. Translations like the New International Version and Christian Standard Bible express the sense of the Greek text far better—Christ is "the firstborn over all creation." However, if I do not know biblical Greek, I could easily be confused by some of the respected translations. If I became aware that some translations use "over" instead of "of," I would not be able to determine which translation was better apart from some acquaintance with Greek grammar and syntax.

ENRICHED BIBLICAL THEOLOGY

For a good example of the value of knowledge of biblical languages for enriching our understanding of biblical theology, we need look no further than the very first phrase of the New Testament. Although many translations suggest that Matthew opened his Gospel with the phrase "the book [or account] of the genealogy of Jesus Christ," this does not fully express the richness of Matthew's Greek expression. You will probably be surprised to know that of all the hundreds of occurrences of the key term in the phrase in ancient Greek texts (57 in the LXX alone), our standard lexica list only one text in which the term may mean "genealogy," and it is this one. In other words, if Matthew's expression refers to a genealogy, he is using the expression in an unusual way distinct from the rest of ancient Greek literature, not to mention biblical literature. When used in the plural, the noun may refer to the generations in a genealogy, but the noun does not refer to a genealogy. The Greek terms for genealogy are *genealogēma, katagōgē*, and *genealogia* (Titus 3:9). Older versions like Tyndale's translation and the King James Version followed the Latin Vulgate and translated the phrase "the book of the generation." Properly understood, this is an accurate translation. But many interpreters seem to have missed that the word refers to a single act of generation, not to the many generations that constitute a genealogy.

Matthew's phrase consists of the noun *biblos,* which means "book" (our word "Bible" is derived from the Greek word), and the noun *geneseos,* which is the genitive form of the noun *genesis*. Thus, the phrase may be translated "The Book of Genesis." "Genesis" was the name for the first book of Moses in the earliest manuscripts of the Septuagint. Philo of Alexandria, a contemporary of Jesus and Matthew, also used this name to refer to the first OT book. Matthew, a careful student of the Old Testament, was undoubtedly aware that this precise phrase appeared in Genesis 2:4 and 5:1, where it introduced the account of the creation of the heavens and the heaven and the account of the creation of humanity, respectively. Matthew is intentionally introducing his Gospel as a creation account like the book of Genesis, and like Genesis 2:4 and 5:1 specifically. The phrase "of Jesus Christ" identifies Jesus as the Creator who brings about this new Genesis, the author of this new creation. This doctrine of new creation appears at several points in Matthew's Gospel. The clearest example is Matthew 19:28, in which Jesus describes the era in which the Son of Man sits on his glorious throne granting eternal life to his disciples as the *palingenesia*: "the regeneration," the "new beginning," "new Genesis," or as the CSB translates, "the renewal of all things." Thus, before Matthew describes Jesus as the virgin-born Immanuel, he titles his Gospel as a book of Genesis, a Genesis performed by Jesus Christ demonstrating that he is the agent of creation and the author of new creation. Jesus will create a new humanity by imparting God's Spirit to give new life to those who were spiritually dead, and he will create a new heaven and earth at the time of his glorious return. Although most Bible readers have probably never heard this interpretation, many and perhaps even most commentators who base their exegesis on the Greek text rather than merely an English translation affirm it. The interpretation seems odd or idiosyncratic because so few Bible teachers know Greek and can consult the best resources.

ABERRANT CHURCH PRACTICES

Baptists affirm that the believer experiences the baptism of the Spirit at the moment of regeneration, the reception of new birth. The primary effect of this spiritual baptism is the cultivation of Christian character and conformity to the image of Christ (*Baptist Faith and Message* II, IV). However, Apostolic Faith Churches hold that the baptism of the Spirit follows both regeneration and sanctification. "When this infilling occurs, it is accompanied by the same sign as the disciples had on the Day of Pentecost—the speaking with 'other tongues, as the

Spirit gave them utterance.'"[4] Similarly, the United Pentecostal Church International teaches:

> The saving gospel is the good news that Jesus died for our sins, was buried, and rose again. We obey the gospel (II Thessalonians 1:8; I Peter 4:17) by repentance (death to sin), water baptism in the name of Jesus Christ (burial), and the baptism of the Holy Spirit with the initial sign of speaking in tongues as the Spirit gives the utterance (resurrection). (See I Corinthians 15:1–4; Acts 2:4, 37–39; Romans 6:3–4.)[5]

Does the New Testament teach that all spiritually mature believers will speak in tongues or that the sign of obedience to the gospel is speaking in tongues? In 1 Corinthians 12:30, the apostle Paul poses a similar question. The ESV translates the questions, "Do all possess gifts of healing? Do all speak with tongues? Do all interpret?" Most major translations handle the verse in a similar fashion (compare NIV, CSB). The translations imply that Paul was asking an open-ended question, and the answer can only be inferred by a careful reading of the context. However, Greek authors could pose binary (yes or no) questions in a variety of ways. A question without the negative did not hint at an implied response. A question with the negative *ouk* implied an affirmative response. A question with the negative *mē* implied a negative response. Paul used the negative *mē*, implying a negative reply. The sense is captured well in the NET, "Not all have gifts of healing, do they? Not all speak in tongues, do they? Not all interpret, do they?"

---

4. Apostolic Faith Church, "Our Beliefs," https://www.apostolicfaith.org/our-faith.

5. United Pentecostal Church International, "Our Beliefs," https://upci.org/our-beliefs.

PRESSING MORAL ISSUES

Knowledge of biblical languages is also crucial for defining Christian morality and ethics in a culture with rapidly shifting values. For example, 1 Corinthians 6:9 describes the wicked who will not inherit the kingdom of God. Two of these categories have been translated in confusing or even misleading ways in the history of the English Bible. In 1526, Tyndale used the translation "weaklings" and "abusars of them selves with the mankynde." In 1560 the Geneva Bible used "wanton" and "buggerers." The King James translators used "effeminate" and "abusers of themselves with mankind." Although modern readers may be puzzled by the expressions in these early translations, commentators recognized that one of the terms referred to "Sodomites," those who committed the sin of the men of Sodom described in Genesis 19 and Jude 7.[6]

The first use of the terms "homosexual" and "heterosexual" appeared in a letter written in German by Karl Maria Kertbeny in 1868. By 1946, the term "homosexual" was used frequently enough in English to describe same-sex sexual acts that the translators of the Revised Standard Version used the word "homosexual" in an English Bible translation for the first time. Despite some recent claims, the translators did not impose the prohibition of sexual relationships between those of the same sex on the Bible. They were merely the first to use the relatively new term "homosexual" in Bible translation. Several authors and filmmakers have perpetrated the myth that the

6. See, for example, Matthew Henry's *Expositions of the Old and New Testaments* (1708–1710) and Matthew Poole's *Synopsis Criticorum* (1669). Poole interprets the second category as "such as are guilty of the sin of Sodom, a sin not to be named among Christians or men."

1946 translators were guilty of a "grave mistranslation" that sparked the "antigay movement among Christians in the United States."[7]

To see precisely what Paul meant in 1 Corinthians 6:9, we need to examine the Greek nouns that he employed. Paul probably coined the last term in the verse, the noun *arsenokoites.* Paul's use of the term here is the earliest in extant Greek literature. Paul will use the term again in 1 Timothy 1:10. The next known usage of the term does not occur until the end of the second century in the writings of Clement of Alexandria. Paul did not coin the term in a linguistic vacuum. Paul formed the word by combining the word *arsen* ("male") with the word *koite* ("bed"). The word refers to "one who goes to bed with a male." Since "bed" was often used as a euphemism for sexual relationships, the term refers to "one who has sex with a male." Paul's term was derived from Leviticus 18:22 ("You are not to sleep with a man as with a woman; it is detestable") and 20:13 ("If a man sleeps with a man as with a woman, they have both committed a detestable act"). The Greek translation (LXX) of these two texts from Leviticus uses both the terms "male" (*arsen*) and "bed/sex" (*koite*), the components of Paul's term. Paul's term forms a clear allusion to these two texts and refers to a man who has sex with a male who fulfills the role ordinarily assumed by a female. Paul's noun in 1 Corinthians 6:9 describes the one who plays the masculine or dominant role in a homosexual act.

The following term in the text is clearer and enables us to precisely define what Paul meant by the preceding term. The word refers to the one who played the *passive* role in a

---

7. *1946: The Mistranslation that Shifted Culture*, written by Jena Serbu, directed by Sharon Roggio, https://www.1946themovie.com/.

homosexual relationship. The term *malakos* (lit. "soft one") was equivalent to the terms *eromenos* (Greek) and *pathicus* or *cinaedus* (Latin). The term was used by ancient writers like Philo to describe the male who played the passive or feminine role in a homosexual act (*Spec. Laws* 3.7 §§37–42; *Dreams* 2.2 §9). The most popular form of homosexuality in the Greco-Roman world was pederasty, in which an older, wealthier male used a younger male (normally under the age of eighteen) for sexual purposes and granted him favors for the relationship. Leading Greek philosophers like Socrates were pederasts and wrote in defense of the practice. The Greek practice eventually infiltrated the Roman Republic. Paul is clearly referring here to the typically younger, feminine partner in a homosexual relationship. Paul prohibited playing the dominant role *and* playing the passive role in a homosexual relationship because Leviticus 20:13 insists "both have committed a detestable act." Many modern interpreters argue that Paul is referring exclusively to abusive homosexual acts, not loving and mutually voluntary homosexual acts. However, if this were so, he would not have condemned the passive partner (who is typically portrayed in current discussions as the object of violence and abuse) along with the dominant partner. Paul's insistence on the wickedness of playing either the dominant or passive role in a homosexual act shows that he viewed consensual homosexual acts as sinful because it was a perversion of the created order and God's moral standards for sexual relationships, not based on the assumption that it was always characterized by violence or abuse.

Several English translations such as the NIV and CSB capture the sense of the text well by merging the two categories: "males who have sex with males." They add a footnote indicating Paul's Greek expression refers to "both passive and active participants in homosexual acts." The ERV preserves the distinction in the two categories and translates: "men who let other men use them for sex or who have sex with other men."

Sadly, Christians are increasingly confused by various translations of this verse that fail to clearly express the meaning of Paul's terms. The RSV originally translated *arsenokoitai* as "homosexual," then changed the translation in 1971 to "sexual pervert." The NRSV of 1989 used the translation "Sodomite." The NRSV updated version of 2021 changed the translation to the more ambiguous wording "men who engage in illicit sex." However, since "illicit" often means "illegal" and "unlawful," readers will assume that homosexual acts that are not criminal are permissible, as if Paul intended Roman law to define the sexual ethics of the church. Since the adjective "illicit" does not appear anywhere else in the translation, even careful readers will struggle to understand precisely what the translators meant by "illicit sex." This ambiguity is intentional since a note adds: "meaning of Gk uncertain."

Since some translations render texts like this that address important moral issues in confusing ways, having a knowledge of biblical languages is crucial for addressing the challenges of our increasingly decadent culture.

CONCLUSION

Knowledge of the Holy Scriptures is essential to Christian ministry. Ministries like evangelism, church planting, cross-cultural missions, counseling, teaching, and preaching require an accurate understanding of the Bible. Since biblical illiteracy is alarmingly widespread even among faithful church attenders, the study of the Bible by candidates for ministry is more important than ever before for the health of the Christian church in America.

The most helpful tool for Bible study is knowledge of the biblical languages: Hebrew and Greek. The ability to look beyond English translations to the original text will help defend the essential truths of the Christian gospel, enrich understanding of biblical theology, and respond to the moral and ethical challenges of a culture that increasingly seeks to redefine biblical standards to justify personal preferences.

Read and Reflect: 2 Timothy 2:1–7

Prayer: *Lord, you have given us air to breathe, words to speak, hearts to love, and minds to think. Help us to steward these gifts to the best of our ability out of love for you and our neighbor. Through Jesus Christ, our Lord. Amen.*

4

BIBLE EXPOSITION FOR MINISTRY PREPARATION

Jim Shaddix

"Of Issachar, men who had understanding of the times, to know what Israel ought to do." Several years ago, I heard these words from 1 Chronicles 12:32 cited and applied by four different ministry leaders in three different contexts in the span of about two weeks.[1] One of them was arguably the most influential pastor in the evangelical world at the time. Another was a seminary professor who referenced the passage in a book he wrote on the same subject. The other two were ministry students presenting papers on the same subject in a seminary classroom. They all basically said the same thing: If we are going to know how to preach, teach, and minister effectively to the current generation, we must be like the men of Issachar and understand our audience and know how they think so we will be able to tell them what to do.

A quick perusal of 1 Chronicles 12 and its context, however, tells a different story. What time was it? It was time to turn the

1. Scripture references in this chapter are from the English Standard Version.

kingdom of Israel over to David from Saul, who had defaulted on the throne (compare 1 Chr 10:13–14). What was Israel supposed to do? They were to support that transition (compare 1 Chr 11:3, 10; 12:23, 38). How did the men of Issachar know what to tell them to do? It was not because they understood the Israelites and knew how they thought, but because they received their instructions from "the word of the Lord" (1 Chr 11:3, 10; 12:23; compare 10:14). Because those four individuals were ministry leaders and they referenced the Bible, their audiences understood them to be saying what God says! However, while what they said may be helpful advice, it is not what God said, at least not in that text. If he said anything, it is that we know what to say to people by knowing what he says in his word!

Putting words in God's mouth or twisting his words to say what we want to say is a profoundly serious matter (see Jer 23:16–32). Whether it is preaching to a congregation, teaching a small group Bible study, writing Bible study curriculum, or giving biblical counsel to hurting people, God expects ministry leaders to get his words right and communicate them accurately. He expects us to be men and women of Issachar—who expound the Bible carefully, "according to the word of the Lord." Doing so demands we have an accurate perception of Bible exposition, understand its prominent place in life and ministry, and make it a priority in theological education.

WHAT BIBLE EXPOSITION IS AND IS NOT

I once heard an interview of a well-known ministry leader who was a vocal critic of expository preaching and teaching. He was asked why he opposed the practice. The man quickly rattled off a litany of reasons for his dislike. When he finished, the interviewer responded with an insightful observation. He said, "You're not opposed to exposition; you're opposed to *poor* exposition." The pastor's perception of Bible exposition was based on abuses of the practice, not careful and skillful demonstrations of it. If we are going to practice Bible exposition in ministry, it is especially important for us and the people we shepherd to have a correct perception of it.

Like the critical ministry leader, all of us have been guilty of throwing the baby out with the bathwater. We reject certain things, not because they are innately flawed, but because we have seen them practiced poorly. For example, one misconception of expository preaching and teaching is that it is characterized by "deep" study that is academic and stuffy. And it is true that Bible communicators who attempt to explain every detail of the language and background of a Bible text—without consideration of their bearing on the meaning of the text—run the risk of overwhelming and even boring their audiences. When teachers include in their messages everything they have discovered in preparation, it is easy for listeners to get lost and lose interest.

Some people shortsightedly limit Bible exposition to working through Bible books. While that practice certainly can be a great way to do exposition, it can also become a nightmare for listeners if it is not done well. Lengthy series without breaks can feel monotonous. Small groups and congregations can become impatient and lose interest if book series are not organized purposefully and navigated prudently. Bad experiences with such practices can turn listeners off.

Another misconception about exposition is that it ignores the Holy Spirit's leadership. After preaching halfway through a Bible book in one of my pastorates, a church member told me that I was not getting my messages from God because I just picked up each week where I left off the previous week. While I hope his conclusion was merely shortsighted, we *can* abuse Bible exposition if we do not choose our series texts prayerfully or present the messages without being utterly dependent on the Spirit's power. Doing so can hinder listeners from sensing the gravity and authority of God's voice and experiencing his supernatural word burning in their hearts (compare Luke 24:27–32).

All these abuses and more can create perceptions that are less than accurate. They can undermine people's appreciation for rich exposition that presents God's word rightly, richly, powerfully, and compellingly. It is critical that we know that not everyone approaches our exposition with a favorable perception, and we must lovingly and carefully shepherd them to appreciate its value.

My uncle is a great bass fisherman, almost annoyingly so. He can catch fish when the fish are not biting and no one else is catching anything. I remember fishing with him one time when I was a boy. It was hot, and the fish were not biting. After a while, I noticed my uncle jerk his rod and set his hook in what he claimed to be a "nice one." I ran along the shore of the lake and arrived just as he pulled a large glob of moss on the bank. I was so disappointed! "It's just moss," I said. He immediately responded, "No, it is a bass. Let me show you." He knelt beside the large lump and began to peel back the nasty, stringy, green strands. As he did, a large, shiny bass appeared!

That day, my uncle did some freshwater exposition for the rest of us. We were there to catch fish, and he caught one. But while reeling it in, it traveled through a bed of moss that latched on and covered up the fish. By the time it got to the bank, it was completely concealed to the point that we did not even know it was there. But he knew. And he did the work of peeling back the layers and exposing the fish, the prize that all the rest of us were hoping we would catch that day! That is the task of Bible exposition—peeling back the layers and exposing the treasure to people—not the treasure of a nasty, smelly fish, but the riches of God's transforming word!

As it has traveled through the centuries, God's revelation has been covered up with a lot of stuff—eons of time, differing cultures, multiple languages and forms of literature, varieties of contexts, numerous and varied human authors, and more. By the time it arrives in the canon of inspired Scripture on the riverbanks of where our people live, it often seems like a glob of chaos they do not understand. Below those layers, however, lies the treasure of God's truth! And it is the only thing that can transform their lives. So, he has ordained that preachers, teachers, counselors, authors, curriculum writers, and other gospel ministry leaders do the work of peeling back the moss and exposing the prize to people so they can experience and enjoy all its benefit (compare Ps 19).

God's people must have an accurate perception of Bible exposition so they can approach it expectantly. I like to define exposition as *the process of laying open a text of Scripture in such a way that the Holy Spirit's intended meaning and accompanying power are brought to bear on the lives of contemporary listeners.* It is the practice of exposing people to what God intended them to hear when he inspired the Bible. In his Spirit's power, we read it carefully, explain it accurately, and exhort them to embrace it enthusiastically (see Neh 8:1–12; 1 Tim 4:13). And when both proclaimers and listeners of the word perceive Bible exposition that way, it becomes more than just a sermon, Bible lesson, curriculum piece, commentary, or word of counsel.

THE PLACE OF BIBLE EXPOSITION IN LIFE AND MINISTRY

The expression "Where the rubber meets the road" refers to the point at which something's validity is put to the test. For example, a boxer can train with a punching bag for years, but the rubber meets the road when he finally gets in the ring with another boxer and finds out how good he really is. Bible exposition may sound like a good practice in a lecture or a textbook, but its true value is not realized until the rubber meets the road of real life and ministry.

When COVID-19 shut the world down in March 2020, kids could not go to school, adults had to work from home, people could not get on airplanes, streets cleared out, and churches started meeting online and on lawns, if at all. It was that last one that created a personal crisis in my life. For thirty-five years, I had been blessed to have a sermon to prepare almost every week. And those weekly responsibilities drove me into God's word to do the work of Bible exposition. But overnight the preaching assignments dried up for several months. Because churches were not gathering, nobody needed interim pastors, supply preachers, or conference speakers. So, for the first time in many years, I did not have the ministry motivation that had driven me into God's word. During those weeks, God graciously and tenderly pursued me with a piercing question: *Do I love him enough to study his word diligently—not because I am a preacher who has a sermon to prepare, but simply because I am his child and need to know him more?*

I was reminded in those weeks that Bible exposition is not primarily a responsibility of my ministry calling, but a responsibility—and privilege—of my salvation calling. God gently reminded me that if I never preached another sermon, taught another Bible study, wrote another commentary, or offered any more biblical counsel, I still needed to regularly interpret, internalize, and apply his word in my own life. I needed to know him and be re-created into Christ's image. I am challenged by the resolve of Ezra, one of Israel's faithful teachers of Scripture: "For Ezra had set his heart to study the Law of the Lord, and to do it and to teach his statutes and rules in Israel" (Ezra 7:10). Ezra studied God's word first because it was God's word, and he needed to align his life with it regardless. Only then was he able to teach it to others.

If we do Bible exposition first as a ministry responsibility, it eventually will become stagnant and academic. But if we do it first because we are God's children and want to know him and obey his voice, it will be a living, vibrant, fruitful, and life-transforming journey for us. And on top of its personal benefit and blessing, it will lift our public ministries to new heights. I do not want to study the Bible because I must preach; I want to preach because I study the Bible. The same thing must be true for our teaching, counseling, and other instructional ministries as well. The value of Bible exposition begins with its necessity and benefit in my personal life as God's child.

BIBLE EXPOSITION IN MINISTRY LEADERSHIP

It had to be incredible to be in that synagogue in Capernaum when Jesus began His public ministry. The people "were astonished at his teaching, for he taught them as one who had authority, and not as the scribes" (Mark 1:22). Mark was not commenting on Jesus's confident voice, persuasive tone, or impressive Old Testament knowledge. He was describing something more. He was describing the people's sense that something supernatural was going on in the room, something out of this world. So, their conclusion was, "That guy's not from around here!"

When we communicate God's word, we want people to hear a voice other than our own. We want them to hear God's voice. As Bible exposition begins to affect us on a personal level, it opens the door for the people we instruct to experience God's word in an otherworldly way. It changes our preaching, teaching, counseling, and writing from being just the mere transference of information between a speaker and an audience to a living encounter with God. The preaching event becomes more than a sermon; the small group study becomes more than a lesson; the word of counsel becomes more than a session; the article, book, and blog become more than mere informational pieces. Our communication becomes the vehicle through which God speaks, and people hear his voice! And that encounter positions them to be transformed by gospel truth.

All truth is God's truth, but God did not ordain all his truth to be part of inspired Scripture known as the Bible. It is true that gravity attracts things toward the earth's center, and that truth certainly belongs to God, who created heaven and earth. But the truth about gravity is not going to re-create anyone into Christ's image for which they were created (compare Gen 1:26, 27; Rom 8:28–30; 2 Cor 3:17–18; 1 John 3:2–3). That transformation only happens through the gospel, which is revealed from Genesis to Revelation in the Bible. And God has ordained his truth in Scripture to be the primary agent the Holy Spirit uses to foster that re-creative transformation in people's lives.

When God's word is interpreted correctly, communicated clearly, delivered powerfully, and received humbly, it does that transforming work in people's lives at the hands of God's Spirit. So, as God's vessels, we must approach our preparation and proclamation in view of that purpose. And we want to lead God's people to come expectantly to corporate worship, personal devotions, small group Bible studies, counseling sessions, and other times and places where the Bible is going to be encountered. For the people of God in the community of faith, Bible exposition must become a practice and event in which we expect God to speak, anticipate his presence, and look and long to know him more. In our various ministry leadership capacities, we can and should approach Bible exposition as an experience through which God reveals Jesus to his people and after which we look more like him than we did when we arrived.

BIBLE EXPOSITION IN MISSIONAL LIVING

One of the main things that attracted me to Southeastern Seminary is its Great Commission focus. I was impressed that it was not just the evangelism and missions professors who were committed to that task. The professors who taught theology, philosophy, biblical studies, counseling, preaching, Christian education, and every other discipline were consumed by it as well. Southeastern's mission is *To glorify the Lord Jesus Christ by equipping students to serve the Church and fulfill the Great Commission.* That is why we strive for every classroom to be a Great Commission classroom. We believe every Christian is on the planet for that purpose.

Such a culture really should not surprise any of us. The Bible is clear that the Great Commission is what Jesus left us here to do. It is really a Great Commission book from beginning to end. The gospel and its proclamation run from start to finish. The gospel is introduced early when God creates humanity in his image to share his life and show his glory (compare Gen 1:16–27). That image is quickly marred, however, when Adam and Eve sin. But God immediately announces to the serpent that he will "put enmity between you and woman, and between your offspring and her offspring; he shall bruise your head, and you shall bruise his heel" (Gen 3:15). And that promise previews the spiritual battle that would be settled in the Christ event.

Then, the Bible ends with John telling us that God's servants "will see his face" (Rev 22:4) and be fully re-created in the image in which they were originally created (compare 1 John 3:1–3). And everything between those bookends is the story of God redeeming his creation by sending his Son to live a life we could not live, die a death we should have died, and rise again to put the life we were created to have—God's life—back inside us. That overarching story of the gospel compels us to live every aspect of our lives through its lens. And in the work of Bible exposition, that grand narrative means that we must help others see where every passage of Scripture stands in relation to Jesus Christ. Bible exposition is Christ-centered and gospel-driven.

Intertwined through that "big picture" theme of the gospel, however, is another theme. It is the companion story of the "mission of God," or the *missio dei*. This Latin term is sometimes translated as the "sending of God." It is the idea that God is sending his servants to carry out his mission of redeeming humanity through the gospel! Like the gospel story, this story also runs from beginning to end in the Bible. Regardless of whether we start with that *protoevangelium*—or first gospel—mentioned above in Genesis 3:15, God's covenant with Noah (Gen 9), or his call and commission of Abram to leave his home so God could make him a blessing to all nations (Gen 12:1–2), we don't have to travel far through the Bible's pages before we're introduced to the mission of God and the sending of his people to proclaim his gospel.

The Bible ends with that mission as well. In its last chapter, the tree of life—from which Adam and Eve had been banned so they would not remain in their unredeemed state (Gen 3:22–24)—appears in heaven "for the healing of the nations" (Rev 22:2; compare 21:26). The Bible's final paragraphs include an invitation for people from every nation to receive God's redemption in Christ: "The Spirit and the Bride say, 'Come.' And let the one who hears say, 'Come.' And let the one who is thirsty come; let the one who desires take the water of life without price" (Rev 22:17). At the beginning and end of the Bible, God's pursuit of his creation rings loudly!

Between those bookends, God's pursuit of the nations is clearly entrusted to his followers. Jesus commissioned us with this task when he charged us to "go therefore and make disciples of all nations" (Matt 28:19). The apostle Paul reiterated this assignment when he claimed, "We are ambassadors for Christ, God making his appeal through us. We implore you on behalf of Christ, be reconciled to God" (2 Cor 5:17). For Christ and the apostles, God's mission was a priority.

What does this theme mean for the task of Bible exposition? Just as with the grand narrative of the gospel, people must be exposed to the companion theme of the Great Commission at every opportunity. We must help them see where relevant passages of Scripture stand in relation to the *missio dei,* the mission and sending of God. We must remind them that if our lives are to be Christ-centered and gospel-driven, then they must be leveraged for the cause of the advancement of that gospel. As God's people hear and see this critical theme repeated when they are taught the Bible, they will have that charge seared into their hearts and their daily lives. They will develop a conviction that to be gospel people means to be missional people. That reality will surface often if their teachers are saying what God says through good Bible exposition.

THE PRIORITY OF BIBLE EXPOSITION IN THEOLOGICAL EDUCATION

If Bible exposition is critical in life and ministry, it logically follows that it must be a priority in the theological training of those who will lead God's people. Years ago, our leadership identified five core competencies that every ministry student should master during their theological training: (1) spiritual formation; (2) biblical exposition; (3) theological integration; (4) ministry preparation; and (5) critical thinking and communication. These competencies appear on every course syllabus along with ways that course aims to help students gain a better grasp of these aptitudes. It is no small thing that when this list was drafted, Bible exposition was included on it. Why? If the right practice of the ministry of God's word is going to be a priority when the rubber meets the road in real life and ministry, it must be a priority in every student's ministry preparation.

BIBLE EXPOSITION IS A PRACTICE IN EVERY CALLING

One of the many manifestations of the westernization of gospel ministry leadership is the creation of a plethora of ministry "callings." When I was growing up the "call to ministry" usually was limited to being a pastor or a missionary. Today, the complexity of the church and its ministries has fostered the evolution of the call to ministry to include a plethora of other areas like worship leadership, student ministry, counseling, church planting, church revitalization, teaching, and many more. Consequently, students are approaching theological education through the lens of a wide variety of ministry callings. And theological colleges and seminaries have sought to accommodate with an equal variety of degree programs, specializations, and tracks.

While I would never say that any of these callings is not a legitimate call from God, I do think the variety and specificity pose a risk of which both students and training institutions need to be aware. The narrower a ministry calling becomes, the easier it is to limit it in nature and scope. And one can limit oneself to the point of giving oneself a pass on certain ministry tasks that God intended to be common to all of us, regardless of specific calling. A preacher like me, for example, might casually excuse himself from getting his hands dirty feeding the hungry or visiting the imprisoned because he must prioritize his preaching. A young woman "called to counseling" might convince herself that her ministry of helping people does not really involve reproductive disciple-making. A young man "called to Christian education" might claim that his ministry of teaching excuses him from personal evangelism. A preacher "called to itinerant evangelism" may become so busy that he justifies his failure to spend unhurried time in prayer.

The risk noted above is true for Bible exposition as well. Throughout this chapter I have tried to provide examples of this task in a variety of ministry expressions like preaching, pastoring, missions, counseling, student ministry, evangelism, Christian education, and more. Regardless of specific calling, every man and woman in ministry leadership will be teaching the Bible in some capacity. Whether it is offering biblical counsel in a formal session, leading a group of men in a Bible study at Starbucks, teaching in a small group, or delivering sermons in a worship service, we all will be ministering God's word in one or more capacities. That means students must be ready to interpret it accurately, communicate it understandably, and apply it relevantly. Because the task of Bible exposition will (or at least should!) show up in every ministry expression, instruction on how to do it well needs to be a part of every theological training curriculum.

BIBLE EXPOSITION IS A PRODUCT OF OTHER DISCIPLINES

Bible exposition is a trainwreck waiting to happen. Think about it. God takes his inerrant, infallible, supernatural word and entrusts it to errant, fallible, natural preachers, teachers, and counselors like us. That makes the Bible interpretation process somewhat subjective. So, the nature of Bible exposition naturally compels us to be utterly dependent on God's Holy Spirit to help us interpret his word in a way that reduces the subjectivity to the greatest degree.

That is why for many years most Bible expositors have championed an approach to Bible interpretation that involves some variation of what has been called the *grammatical-historical-theological* approach. God's revelation was not given in momentary isolation through one means. He used multiple languages, centuries of time, various and progressive deposits of knowledge about himself, numerous literary genres, and many other variables. Consequently, when we interpret the Bible, we reduce the subjectivity best when we consider as many variables as we can: *grammar*, *history*, *theology*, and more. We do not just look at one or two of those, but we consider them all, along with other elements like background, context, and genre. We take all those elements into consideration to rightly discern what God has said in his word.

In a perfect world, Bible exposition courses would be some of the last courses students took in their theological training. The reason for such an idealistic suggestion is because the practice of good Bible exposition is informed by just about all the other disciplines found in theological training. It requires the application of numerous other areas of knowledge and skill. To interpret the Bible correctly and communicate it understandably, we use biblical languages, the Old and New Testaments, systematic and biblical theology, philosophy, history, and more. In utter dependence on the Holy Spirit's help, we use all those disciplines of study and more to spiritually discern what God has inspired so we can carefully communicate it to the people under our care.

But we do not live in a perfect world, which means it is not always possible to order courses of study in theological education in the most ideal sequence. But we can make sure we include and prioritize Bible exposition in the journey, demonstrate in the instruction of other disciplines how each one relates to the exposition of Scripture, and teach Bible exposition in a holistic way that incorporates the other disciplines and shows their importance to the task. Bible exposition is certainly not an end in itself. But neither is it the beginning of ministry leadership. It is the product of all the other disciplines that are part of the theological education journey.

CONCLUSION: THOSE WHO MUST GIVE AN ACCOUNT

One of the most haunting verses in the Bible for me is Hebrews 13:17—"Obey your leaders and submit to them, for they are keeping watch over your souls, as those who will have to give an account. Let them do this with joy and not with groaning, for that would be of no advantage to you." While this verse is an admonition to people who are shepherded by ministry leaders, it clearly declares a frightening reality about our task. I do not know exactly what it is going to look like or when in the eschaton it's going to take place. But if I understand the verse correctly, one day we will have to answer for the condition of the souls of people who were under our care.

In this chapter we have noted that the primary agent God has ordained to nurture the souls of his people and re-create them into his foreordained image is the truth of his word. That makes the right understanding and practice of Bible exposition essential in ministry leadership today. Men and women called to ministry leadership must be equipped to engage God's word personally, interpret it carefully, instruct others in it compellingly, and do all these in utter dependence on the Spirit's help. To make this happen, Bible colleges, seminaries, and local churches must partner together to prepare ministry leaders to be men and women who are ready "to give an account" for the souls of those entrusted to their care through the work of Bible exposition.

Read and Reflect: Acts 17:1–4

Prayer: *God, who showed your love for us by the death of Christ on the cross, help us to preach and teach your gospel faithfully from your word. Grant us the time and resources, the heart and the mind, to love your Scriptures, study them earnestly, and communicate them clearly. Through Jesus Christ, our Lord. Amen.*

5

PHILOSOPHY FOR MINISTRY PREPARATION

Ben Holloway

In his *Republic,* Plato contends that philosophers ought to rule as kings.[1] In a seminary, it is the reverse. In a seminary, a philosopher serves. As Christian philosopher Alvin Plantinga writes, "Christian philosophers . . . are the philosophers of the Christian community; and it is part of their task as Christian philosophers to serve the Christian community."[2]

Christian philosophy is fundamentally a humble task whose purpose is to serve the Lord and his ministers. No less is a seminary student's knowledge of philosophy a necessary servant to the task of ministry. In this chapter, I will explain what philosophy is and its role in the life to which God has called us.

WHAT PHILOSOPHY IS

The word *philosophy* means "love of wisdom." It is associated with the Greek enlightenment beginning in the sixth century BC.

---

1. Plato, *Republic* 474b–c.

2. Alvin Plantinga, "Advice to Christian Philosophers," *Faith and Philosophy* 1 (1984): 255.

It was an era during which amazing advances were made in science, history, politics, sport, and the arts. Philosophy now has a narrower definition, but it remains a *love.* It stems from a desire to know about God's world.

In our contemporary context, philosophy has an even narrower definition. It is the pursuit of answers to difficult, logically fundamental questions that have far-reaching consequences. Some questions are about the nature of the world. What kinds of things exist? What is time? Do we have free will? What is a human person? All these questions are usually categorized as *metaphysical* questions. They are about what is *really* real.

Other questions are about knowledge. What can we know? What makes the difference between believing something and knowing it? What is truth? Other questions are about ethics. What makes an action right or wrong? What do we mean by "good"? How do we justify our moral beliefs?

It is difficult to know how to answer any of these questions. Consequently, philosophers have developed a high degree of skill in logic. Logic is the study of arguments. What kinds of arguments are there, and what makes them good or bad?

In addition, there are all sorts of fascinating philosophical questions about science, religion, theology, art, education, history, law, politics, economics, and language. These kinds of questions are called *second-order* questions. Philosophy of religion, the primary philosophical degree offered by seminaries, is a second-order discipline. Philosophers of religion seek to answer questions about the relationship between faith and reason, arguments for the existence of God, the problem of evil, the coherence of concepts of God and ultimate reality, the defensibility of miracles, and the problem of religious pluralism.

Having understood what philosophy is, we can turn to its use in our ministry. J. P. Moreland and William Lane Craig provide a list of ways philosophy aids us to serve the cause of Christ.[3]

PHILOSOPHY HELPS OUR APOLOGETIC

> In your hearts regard Christ the Lord as holy, ready at any time to give a defense to anyone who asks you for a reason for the hope that is in you. —1 Peter 3:15

First, thinking through those kinds of questions helps us meet our obligation to give reasons for our hope. For example, consider some objections to the Christian faith. Suppose someone claims that there isn't enough evidence to believe that God exists, or that the Bible is true, or that Jesus rose from the dead. Complaints about evidence require understanding what kinds of reasons are sufficient for beliefs, and how to construct good arguments in their favor.

Jesus took evidence seriously. He criticized both those who refused to form beliefs on the basis of good evidence and those who took even the poorest evidence to be sufficient for a belief. For example, he told his intransigent opposition that they had been given more than enough evidence for his messiahship and would be held accountable for their disbelief (Matt 11:20–24). He also speaks poorly of those who are easily swayed by popular opinion (Luke 7:24; Matt 11:7).

Other objections require us to know how to defend the *consistency* of our beliefs. For example, someone might suggest that we *can't* rationally believe that God is all good and all powerful given that there is evil in the world. In reply, we must be able

3. Plantinga, "Advice to Christian Philosophers," 255.

to show how all our beliefs fit together without committing ourselves to contradictions.

PHILOSOPHY HELPS OUR POLEMICS

> Be careful that no one takes you captive through philosophy and empty deceit based on human tradition, based on the elements of the world, rather than Christ. —Colossians 2:8

In his letter to the Colossians, Paul warns that some people might try to capture Christians and carry them away from the faith. In Paul's day, many people earned a living from their forceful speech. If they were effective, they could captivate an audience and "carry them away." Paul says that some of these powerful speakers used worldly philosophy to attempt to capture the minds of Christians to worldly thinking. Hence, we should beware of those people.

As ministers we are tasked with protecting ourselves and our brothers and sisters from false views or even heresies propagated by forceful leaders. Protection requires more than merely warning others. We should also be able to *rationally refute* falsity, showing where arguments for false views go wrong.[4]

For example, philosophy helps provide reasons to reject relativism, the view that there are no truths or reasons to believe anything independent of our cultures or individual perspectives. According to relativists, beliefs are generated merely by one's autobiography, psychology, or society. Beliefs and our means of assessing them are a result of a local culture and way of life. We can't challenge them by appealing to truth or universal rules of reason. Hence, they aren't rationally assessable.

---

4. J. P. Moreland and William Lane Craig, *Philosophical Foundations for a Christian Worldview*, 2nd ed. (Downers Grove, IL: IVP Academic, 2017), 17.

Such a view is deeply damaging to Christian witness in the world. Refuting it is a necessary precursor to presenting a case for Christian beliefs.

PHILOSOPHY HELPS OUR DOGMATICS

> Be diligent to present yourself to God as one approved, a worker who doesn't need to be ashamed, correctly teaching the word of truth. —2 Timothy 2:15

Further questions are raised internally by our own Christian beliefs. Moreland and Craig list three ways in which philosophy aids our theological task. First, philosophy serves the theological task by clarifying theological concepts and statements.[5] Often the Bible clearly teaches a doctrine but doesn't explain how it can be true. For example, the Bible clearly supports the view that God is supremely powerful. Jeremiah writes, "Oh, Lord God! You yourself made the heavens and the earth by your great power and with your outstretched arm. Nothing is too difficult for you!" (Jer 32:17). We worship *all*-mighty God. However, working out what the concept of omnipotence amounts to and how it applies to God requires a process of clarification in the face of a series of counterexamples.

One must have a concept of omnipotence that applies to God but that also rules out God being able to sin or do anything logically impossible. It also must rule out the omnipotence of other beings. Omnipotence is a possession of God and no other. The definition also ought to be able to tell us why God cannot make a rock so big that he cannot lift it. Whatever analysis is provided, it must be logically coherent and consistent with what the Bible teaches.

---

5. Moreland and Craig, *Philosophical Foundations*, 17.

Second, philosophers attempt to "extend biblical teaching into areas where the Bible isn't explicit."[6] In ethics, philosophers attempt to derive principles to deal with advances in technology, health care, and culture. For example, though the Bible does not mention in vitro fertilization (IVF), we can derive principles from it that, in turn, can form the basis of a view on the matter.[7]

Finally, Moreland and Craig note how important philosophy has been for enhancing the study of the Bible. A vital component of ministry is rightly interpreting Scripture (2 Tim 2:15). But what does it mean to rightly interpret anything? What is it that we are looking for when we try to find the meaning of a text? Who or what fixes or determines its meaning? How many meanings can a text have? These sorts of philosophical questions are vitally important. If we get them wrong, we won't know what God has to say to us through his word.

In addition to formulating our biblical beliefs clearly, coherently, and faithfully, having a minimal understanding of philosophy will also help us understand the great theologians of the past. We understand Augustine better if we understand Plato; we understand Aquinas better if we understand Aristotle; we understand much modern liberal theology better if we understand Kant and Hegel; we understand progressive postmodern theology better if we grasp the central tenets of postmodern philosophy, and so on.[8]

---

6. Moreland and Craig, *Philosophical Foundations*, 17.

7. For example, see John Feinberg and Paul Feinberg, *Ethics for a Brave New World* (Wheaton, IL: Crossway, 2010), 406–32.

8. For example, see Diogenes Allen and Eric Springsted, *Philosophy for Understanding Theology* (Louisville: Westminster John Knox, 2007).

PHILOSOPHY HELPS OUR WORSHIP

> For none of us lives for himself, and no one dies for himself. If we live, we live for the Lord; and if we die, we die for the Lord. Therefore, whether we live or die, we belong to the Lord. Christ died and returned to life for this: that he might be Lord over both the dead and the living. —Romans 14:7–9

Philosophy serves not only by aiding the task of answering difficult questions. It also helps us use what the Lord has given us for his glory. As Dr. Ross Inman argues, philosophy hasn't always been a purely theoretical discipline. Instead, ancient philosophers, both Christian and non-Christian, saw philosophy as a therapeutic discipline, a way to a good life.[9] Consequently, "studying philosophy can actually change your life."[10]

First, as Moreland and Craig point out, philosophy aids the expression of the image of God in the lives of Christians. God has given us rationality to use for his purposes. We should train ourselves to use what he has given to its greatest measure. Thinking rationally, ethically, and deeply about the most fundamental questions of truth, reality, and values is to use one's mental faculties at the highest level, getting the most out of what God has given us.

Second, in our present era, we are going to need courage to defend the gospel publicly. The kind of courage cannot be born of self-interested pride. Instead, it must be a "*Christian* courage, or boldness, or strength, or perhaps Christian self-confidence."[11] Christian courage is uniquely humble. It is done in the service

---

9. Ross Inman, *Christian Philosophy as a Way of Life* (Grand Rapids: Baker Academic, 2023), 39.

10. Inman, *Christian Philosophy as a Way of Life*, 169.

11. Plantinga, "Advice to Christian Philosophers," 254, emphasis mine.

of God and the people to whom he has called us. As Moreland and Craig point out, philosophy helps enhance our confidence in the world. "Because of the very nature of philosophy itself—its areas of study and their importance for answering ultimate questions, the questions it asks and answers, its closeness to theology—the potential of this discipline for enhancing the self-respect of the believing community is enormous."[12]

This is as true now as it was in the time of Justin Martyr, Origen, and Tertullian. Philosophical skills are very demanding! So, developing them will give us more power to contribute to our own Christian community and more confidence in presenting what we believe to an often hostile world.

Developing confidence based on our reasoning skills will also help us avoid character pitfalls. If we lack the capacity to make a case for what we believe, we will likely either be fearful and easily led, or closed-minded and overly confident. As Greg Welty points out, those kinds of pitfalls make us unable to serve others as we ought. On the topic of apologetics, he writes,

> Useful Christian apologetics is incompatible with two kinds of people: the fearful and the over-confident. The fearful are too afraid to lay their cards on the table, while the over-confident engage in sleight of hand to effect a quick outcome when no one is looking. Both approaches hide the truth, though for different reasons, and so neither approach really makes a case. But anxious secrecy and cynical manipulation have a habit of disappointing people who are really interested in the truth. Make a case! Have faith that you think you can do it ... plan to be persistent in doing it ... think hard about how to

12. Moreland and Craig, *Philosophical Foundations,* 18.

> do it ... and then do your best, being open to correction by others.[13]

Most striking about what Welty says is his insistence that one should make a case to avoid disappointing "people who are really interested in the truth." Christians sometimes worry that developing the capacity to reason well will make us proud. But as Welty points out, case-making should not be pride-inducing. Instead, it is done *in the service of those who are seeking the truth.* It is fundamentally a *humble* task carried out in the interests of others.

If use of our rational faculties helps us make a case for our beliefs, we should also recognize the aid it can play in fairly assessing the cases others make for theirs. In addressing a disagreement with believers or nonbelievers, we ought to be able to understand the reasons they have for their beliefs. Further, we ought to be able to fairly represent those reasons and respond to them without brushing them aside. Being charitable, honest, and open to hearing how other people think demonstrates good character and love for people. Hence, philosophy helps us meet our obligation to reason with others, "with gentleness and reverence, keeping a clear conscience" (1 Pet 3:16).

CAN PHILOSOPHY BE CHRISTIAN?

Some may be concerned that philosophy is somehow *unchristian.* For example, Paul's warning about "philosophy and empty deception" in the above-mentioned verse may be taken to rule out philosophy from a Christian's course of study. Pause should be given over such a conclusion from the fact that the most

13. Greg Welty, "Richard Swinburne," in *The History of Apologetics*, ed. Benjamin Forrest, Joshua Chatraw, and Alistair McGrath (Grand Rapids: Zondervan, 2020), 728–29.

influential theologians in our heritage read and practiced the discipline. Nonetheless, it should also be argued that the verse does not entail that philosophy is forbidden for Christians.

Paul tells us that forceful people will try to capture and carry away Christians to "philosophy and empty deceit." At first glance, it appears that Paul is prohibiting the study of philosophy altogether! However, although "empty deceit" and "philosophy" are conjoined, not all conjunctions are used for lists. They can also be used to indicate that one word is modifying the other. Taken this way, Paul's phrase should probably read "empty, deceitful philosophy" (see the NET translation for an example of this way of translating the phrase). If so, then philosophy itself isn't bad, even if some of it is empty and deceitful.

Further, Paul goes on to answer the question, "What kind of philosophy should we avoid?" by saying, "According to men, according to the basic principles of the world, and not according to Christ." His point is not that all philosophies are somehow intrinsically dishonoring to the Lord, but that some of them are.

Worldly philosophies are different now than they were in Paul's time. But Paul's exhortation is still a good one. Present intellectual threats to the Christian life include moral relativism or relativism about truth, atheistic commitments, denials of the resurrection, and skepticism about the knowledge of God. Reading philosophy from a Christian perspective should improve our defenses against these ideas. We will also be better equipped to help others avoid being carried away by them.

THEOLOGY AND PHILOSOPHY

If philosophy is supposed to serve ministry, what role does it have in our theological task? Won't studying philosophy *compete* with our study of the Bible? What do we do if we find a good philosophical answer that contradicts the teaching of the Bible? How does the Bible contribute to our philosophical reasoning?

Theologian, ethicist, and philosopher John Feinberg explains how we can answer questions that involve the Bible and other sources such as science or philosophy.[14] Feinberg argues that the most important thing to remember is that the Bible is authoritative on all matters to which it speaks. It follows that the Bible plays two important roles in reasoning. First, for any question, one must start with Scripture. Second, when correctly interpreted, what the Bible says outweighs the deliverances of any other discipline.

If one's study of the Bible has yielded a clear answer to a question, whatever another discipline might add it won't be sufficient to overturn what the Bible teaches. Alternatively, if there is not enough data from the Bible to make a conclusion, then one may weigh in findings from other disciplines, being careful to remain consistent with other clear teachings from the Bible.

Sometimes, one finds that the Bible leaves the question unanswered or creates a tension that it never resolves. In such cases one may look to other disciplines for answers. In these situations, philosophy can play a prominent role. For example, the Bible clearly teaches that God is one divine being. It also teaches that there are three divine persons, the Father, Son, and Holy Spirit. But it doesn't directly teach how it can be possible that God is both one divine being and three divine persons at the same time. Ever since the early church, Christian theologians and philosophers have worked out models of the Trinity more fully that are faithful to the Bible's teaching and also logically coherent. Other examples include reconciling human persons'

14. John Feinberg, *No One like Him: The Doctrine of God* (Wheaton, IL: Crossway, 2001), 579–81.

free will with God's knowledge of their future actions, resolving the problem of evil, and showing how one person can be both divine and human in Jesus Christ.

Feinberg emphasizes that, in answering a question from another discipline, one must always return to the Bible to check that it is consistent with its teachings. In some cases, philosophy may yield several answers, one of which is much better than the others, philosophically speaking. However, when one returns to the "trump card" of Scripture, it turns out that it is inconsistent with what the Bible clearly teaches. In such cases, one must rule out any answers from other disciplines that are inconsistent with Scripture *even if those answers are philosophically better than others.* It is better to have a less plausible philosophical answer than a less scriptural one!

The most important point to remember is that philosophy should serve neither as a competitor to nor as an authority over theology. Instead, philosophy should serve the theological task and, ostensibly, the ministry of the church in the world.

PHILOSOPHY AND OUR MINISTRIES

Perhaps academic theologians have been helped by philosophy, but what can philosophy do for my daily practical ministry? Surely, we could leave the academic side to academics while we focus on the task at hand. Such an unfortunate division is misguided. As Andrew Fuller demonstrated some 250 years ago, where theology goes, missions will surely follow.[15] Indeed, it is difficult to understand what missions would amount to if there is little interest in developing a high degree of knowledge of God's word and his world. We would possess only an

15. John Piper, *Andrew Fuller: Holy Faith, Worthy Gospel, World Mission* (Wheaton, IL: Crossway, 2026), 55–57.

anemic version of the gospel and little capacity to understand the worldviews of those we seek to reach.

Still, one might wonder how *philosophy* has anything to do with practical issues. The Great Commission may require us to do evangelism, missions, counselling, pastoring, teaching, or leading worship, but the Bible makes no mention of a call to be a philosopher! Philosophy may be a good thing to learn in seminary, but after that, when the practical part starts, what need will I have of it then?

First, as Ross Inman ably argues, philosophy is itself a practical discipline.[16] Mental works are no less practical than physical works. Moreover, every physical action will in part be because of a prior mental action. Getting the mind right is the precursor to right action. As Peter instructs us, "Prepare your minds for action" (1 Pet 1:13 ESV).

Aside from the mental activity involved in philosophy itself, it is also an aid to the practical skills required for ministry. Although covering all the applications of philosophy to various ministries would lengthen this chapter beyond a readable limit, here are a few examples.

Those who feel called to Christian counseling will avail themselves of a study of human psychology in order to care rightly for people. However, to care for something would be a frustrating task if one lacked knowledge of its nature. I can't keep my car running if I don't know whether it runs on gas or electric power. Likewise, to care for a human one must know what kind of thing a human is.

The Bible presents a clear anthropology, including the claim that all human beings are made in the image of God (Gen 1:27). The Bible also indicates that persons survive bodily death and

---

16. Inman, *Christian Philosophy as a Way of Life*, 115–33.

have an afterlife. It also informs us of our ultimate problem with sin. But there are some other consequent questions about which philosophy seeks answers.

For example, philosophers provide metaphysical models for what constitutes human persons. Are we just bodies, or minds with bodies, or a single kind of substance with both physical and mental aspects? Whatever position is taken will determine how we treat people in a counselling situation. If we are merely physical bodies, then any attempt to treat a problem will be an attempt to treat a physical object. If we are mental in nature, our attempt to care will be appropriate to embodied minds. As David Entwistle argues, any psychology of a human will involve assuming a philosophical worldview.[17] Having an adequately worked-out philosophy of mind is an essential task for one who seeks to care for people well.

What does philosophy have to do with preaching? Initially, good reasoning will enable a preacher to understand the meaning of a given text. As Paul Helm argues, understanding the meaning of a sentence in the Bible consists of applying logical principles.[18] We understand a sentence if and only if we know the conditions under which it is true; we can restate the meaning of the sentence using other words; we know what logically follows from the sentence; and we know what it doesn't mean. All of those requirements of us are essentially *logical* in nature.

Moreover, logic aids preachers in developing the sermon from the text. Bryan O'Neal expresses a common concern with contemporary preaching when he writes, "The visual and

---

17. David Entwistle, *Integrative Approaches to Psychology and Christianity* (Eugene, OR: Cascade, 2021), 161.

18. Paul Helm, "The Role of Logic in Biblical Interpretation," in *Hermeneutics, Inerrancy, and the Bible: Papers from ICBI Summit II*, ed. Earl Radmacher and Robert Preus (Grand Rapids: Zondervan, 1984), 841.

emotional are enjoying ascendency over the logical and rational."[19] As O'Neal claims, logic aids the preacher to comprehend the reasoning a biblical author is deploying. But it also aids him to present a rationally compelling case for his interpretation of Scripture while avoiding any logical mistakes (fallacies).[20]

Those who wish to serve by using an artform may find some of their questions difficult to answer without some philosophical reflection. What is the purpose of music in a worship service? Is it merely to aid our emotional states as we sing the words? If that isn't its point, what is? What is the role of Christian fiction? Fiction isn't supposed to be true, so what use is it? What of church buildings? Must a building committee consider the aesthetics of a new church building? If so, what is the appropriate "look" they should aim at, and why? Such questions require philosophical reflection on what makes art valuable, what role the emotions and morality should play in Christian artistic endeavor, and the overall relationship between the Christian life and the arts.[21]

Moral issues are also paramount to any role in ministry. The missionary has an especially challenging task in distinguishing between the mores of a culture and what falls under the explicit and implicit prescriptions from God. Christian missionaries are adept at adapting the Christian life to other cultures due to their deep appreciation and love for the people to whom God has called them. But steering such a course correctly requires a concerted effort to understand what makes actions right or

---

19. Bryan O'Neal, "The Logic of the Sermon," in *The Moody Handbook of Preaching*, ed. John Koessler (Chicago: Moody, 2008), 336.

20. For examples of common fallacies plaguing sermons, see D. A. Carson, *Exegetical Fallacies* (Grand Rapids: Baker, 1996).

21. For further philosophical issues in theological aesthetics, see Gordon Graham, *Philosophy, Art, and Religion: Understanding Faith and Creativity* (New York: Cambridge University Press, 2017).

wrong, how one goes about justifying (giving reasons) for the moral status of actions, and being able to avoid implicitly adopting moral relativism when attempting to marry their love for the people they serve with their obligation to preach the gospel, which begins with "all have sinned and fallen short of the glory of God" (Rom 3:23).

Much more could be said about many more practical ministries, but the examples highlighted demonstrate a need for some philosophical reflection for good, life-long Christian ministry.

CONCLUSION

In this chapter, I have intentionally raised many more philosophical questions than I have answered. The answers cannot be stated quickly—almost no important answer ever can be—so they can't fit into a short chapter. They are difficult questions that require lengthy treatments. Pursuing their answers is part of the kind of training we need as those who wish to serve the Lord well. Their answers can be reached by extended reading, discussion, and instruction—the kinds of activities found at seminary.

Read and Reflect: 1 Peter 3:15–16

Prayer: *God of all wisdom and truth, who spoke creation into existence, whose thoughts are higher than our thoughts, give us wisdom, patience, and humility so that our lives might be conformed into Christ. Through Jesus Christ, our Lord. Amen.*

6

CHURCH HISTORY FOR MINISTRY PREPARATION

Steven A. McKinion

At the outset of the COVID-19 pandemic, I heard a pastor say, "Seminary never prepared me for this." While there may not be a seminary class titled, "What to Do When a Worldwide Pandemic Strikes and Churches Are Shut Down," much of a robust theological education is the training that prepares future church leaders and members for countless unforeseeable catastrophes in church life. Courses in church history, historical theology, and the history of Christianity are essential to this training. Students take church history early in their program of study as a foundation for courses such as Christian theology, biblical studies, and hermeneutics. Anyone serious about shaping minds, leading congregations, serving Christians, and explaining to the world why Christianity is important for them and their communities should devote significant time and attention to Church history.

WHY IS CHURCH HISTORY IMPORTANT?

Church history is a treasure trove of wisdom, a vast repository of experiences, ideas, and struggles that have shaped Christian churches for two millennia. For seminary students, delving into this rich historical narrative is not merely an academic exercise; it is a vital component of theological education that informs, guides, and enriches their understanding of the Christian faith. The study of church history provides context to the Baptist tradition, deepens theological knowledge, and fosters a sense of identity and continuity within the broader Christian tradition. By exploring the roots of their denomination, learning from past mistakes and successes, and preparing for global and ecumenical engagement, seminary students can develop a well-rounded and informed approach to ministry. Such study is essential for forming well-equipped, theologically grounded, and historically aware leaders who can navigate contemporary Christian life and ministry complexities.

Like all Christian denominations, the Baptist tradition did not emerge in a vacuum. It is the product of centuries of theological development, social change, and spiritual renewal. To fully appreciate and articulate the distinctives of the faith, seminary students must first understand the historical context from which it arose. The Baptist movement began in the early seventeenth century and was rooted in the broader Protestant Reformation, a time of significant upheaval and reform within Christianity. The Reformation was a response to widespread corruption and doctrinal confusion within the Catholic Church, and it gave rise to various movements seeking to return to what they believed was a more authentic, scriptural Christianity. While many are familiar with the contributions of figures like Luther and Calvin, it is helpful to recognize how early reform efforts shaped the Baptist movement in their quest for theological accuracy and faithfulness to the Bible.

Building on the foundation of the earlier reformers, Baptists developed their own distinct theological emphases. Key figures in the Baptist movement, such as John Smyth and Thomas Helwys, played pivotal roles in shaping Baptist theology and practice. John Smyth, often credited with founding the first Baptist church in 1609, was originally a minister in the Church of England. However, he became increasingly dissatisfied with the state church's practices and its ties to the government. Seeking a more biblical form of church governance, Smyth broke away from the Anglican Church, formed a congregation that practiced believers' baptism, and embraced a congregational form of church government. Smyth's decision to rebaptize himself and his followers was a radical move that underscored the importance of personal faith and the rejection of infant baptism, which he considered unbiblical.

Thomas Helwys further developed these ideas and established the first Baptist congregation in England. Helwys was mainly concerned with religious liberty issues and the state's role in matters of faith. In his landmark work *A Short Declaration of the Mystery of Iniquity* (1612), Helwys argued that the state should not interfere in matters of conscience and that religious freedom should be granted to all individuals, regardless of their beliefs. This was a groundbreaking argument when rulers enforced religious uniformity, and it laid the foundation for the Baptist commitment to religious liberty and the separation of church and state.

The historical developments that shaped the early Baptist movement were not mere theological abstractions; they were responses to specific religious, social, and political contexts. For example, the Baptist emphasis on believers' baptism was a direct challenge to the widespread practice of infant baptism, which they saw as a nonbiblical carryover from Catholic tradition. By insisting that baptism was for those who could consciously profess their faith, the early Baptists declared that the nature of the church was a community of believers rather than a mixed multitude of believers and non-believers. This emphasis on personal faith and conversion aligned with the broader Protestant Reformation's focus on individual faith over institutional affiliation, but it also distinguished Baptists from other Protestants who practiced infant baptism.

Similarly, Baptist commitment to congregational governance reflected a rejection of hierarchical church structures, advocating instead for the autonomy of the local congregation. This practice was a significant departure from the Catholic Church with its highly centralized authority, and from many Protestant denominations who maintained some form of hierarchical oversight. The Baptists believed that each local congregation should be self-governing, with the authority to make decisions about its leadership, worship practices, and membership. This emphasis on regional autonomy was a theological conviction and a practical response to the persecution and marginalization many early Baptists faced from the state and established churches. The Baptists maintained their distinct identity and practices by organizing themselves into independent congregations despite external pressure.

By studying the historical roots of these and other Baptist distinctives, seminary students can better understand why they hold their beliefs and how historical circumstances have shaped them. This understanding is crucial not only for theological clarity but also for effective ministry. For example, understanding the historical reasons behind Baptist emphasis on believers' baptism can help future pastors articulate the significance of this practice in a way that resonates with their congregations and engages contemporary theological debates. Similarly, understanding the historical context of the Baptist commitment to religious liberty and congregational governance can equip seminary students to navigate the challenges of church-state relations and church leadership in today's complex social and political landscape.

THEOLOGICAL DEVELOPMENT AND DOCTRINAL CLARITY

Church history is not just about dates and events but also about ideas—the development of doctrines and theological perspectives that have shaped the Christian faith over centuries. For seminary students, understanding this development is crucial for maintaining doctrinal clarity and engaging thoughtfully with the broader Christian tradition.

Theological debates and controversies are a constant feature of church history, from the early christological debates of the first few centuries to the more recent discussions on the nature of the church, salvation, and the sacraments. These debates have significantly shaped the contours of Christian theology, and the Baptist tradition is no exception.

One of the earliest and most significant theological debates in church history was the christological controversy that culminated in the Council of Nicaea in AD 325. The debate centered on the nature of Christ and his relationship to God the Father, with the critical question being whether Christ was of the same substance (*homoousios*) as the Father or merely of a similar substance (*homoiousios*). The eventual affirmation of Christ's full divinity in the Nicene Creed was a decisive moment in the history of Christian doctrine, establishing a foundational understanding of the Trinity that would influence all subsequent theological developments. For seminary students, studying these early debates is essential for grasping the core tenets of Christian orthodoxy and understanding the historical context in which Christians formulated these doctrines.

As the centuries progressed, the church grappled with various issues, leading to the development of key doctrines that remain central to the Christian faith today. For example, the doctrine of atonement, which concerns how Christ's death on the cross reconciles humanity with God, has been a subject of ongoing theological reflection and debate. Different atonement theories, such as the Christus Victor model, the satisfaction theory, and the moral influence theory, have been proposed throughout church history, emphasizing various aspects of Christ's saving work. By studying these developments, students can deepen their understanding of the multifaceted nature of the atonement and articulate a more robust theology of salvation grounded in the broader Christian tradition.

The Protestant Reformation of the sixteenth century was a watershed moment in church history that profoundly influenced Baptist theology. The Reformers' emphasis on *sola scriptura* (Scripture alone) and *sola fide* (faith alone) resonated deeply with the emerging Baptist movement. These principles became foundational to Baptist theology, which places a high value on the Scripture's authority and the necessity of personal faith. However, the Reformation also introduced new theological debates, such as the nature of the sacraments and the relationship between grace and free will, that would continue to shape the contours of Baptist thought.

A significant area of development within Baptist theology is the role of the local church. Baptist ecclesiology, or the theology of the church, emphasizes congregational governance, where each local church is a self-governing body of believers, contrasted with more hierarchical church structures in other Christian traditions. The Baptist commitment to congregationalism is rooted in the belief that Christ is the head of the church and that each congregation, under the guidance of the Holy Spirit, can discern God's will for its community. This theological conviction has practical implications for how Baptists organize their churches, make decisions, and interact with other congregations. By studying the historical development of Baptist ecclesiology, seminary students can better understand the theological foundations of congregational governance and how it informs Baptist practice today.

The relationship between church and state is a significant area of theological debate within the Baptist tradition. From its earliest days, the Baptist movement advocated for the separation of church and state, arguing that the state should not have the authority to dictate religious beliefs or practices. This conviction was born out of the experiences of religious persecution faced by early Baptists, who were often marginalized and oppressed by both Catholic and Protestant authorities. The Baptist commitment to religious liberty has had a lasting impact on the development of democratic principles and human rights, particularly in the context of American history. Seminary students can better understand the theological rationale behind these principles and their relevance in contemporary discussions about church-state relations by studying the historical struggles for religious freedom.

Church history also provides valuable lessons on the importance of doctrinal clarity. Throughout history, the church has faced numerous challenges from heretical movements that sought to distort or undermine core Christian beliefs. For example, the early church's struggle against heresy led to the development of the Nicene Creed, a foundational statement of Christian orthodoxy. The Arian heresy, which posited that the Son is not coeternal with the Father, threatened to undermine the very basis of the Christian faith. In response, the early church fathers articulated a coherent doctrine of the Trinity, affirming that the Son is eternally begotten and of the same substance as the Father. This doctrinal clarity was essential for preserving the Christian message's integrity and guiding the church through subsequent theological challenges.

Similarly, the Baptist tradition has contended with various theological challenges, from antinomianism to modern-day relativism. Antinomianism, the belief that Christians are not bound by moral law, was a theological threat that arose during the early years of the Baptist movement. This heresy undermined the ethical teachings of Christianity and threatened to lead believers into moral laxity. In response, Baptist theologians emphasized the importance of holy living as a natural outgrowth of genuine faith and a reflection of the gospel's transformative power. By studying how past generations of Christians have defended and articulated their faith in the face of such challenges, students can be better equipped to uphold doctrinal clarity in their ministries.

The study of church history exposes seminary students to other Christian denominations' rich liturgical and spiritual traditions. While Baptists traditionally emphasize a simple and non-liturgical form of worship, learning about the liturgical practices of other traditions can enrich the worship life of Baptist communities. For example, the practice of observing the Christian calendar, with its seasons of Advent, Lent, and Easter, can provide a more profound sense of the rhythm of the Christian life and the unfolding of the gospel story throughout the year. By engaging with these practices, students can find ways to incorporate meaningful elements of the broader Christian tradition into their worship and spiritual practices.

LEARNING FROM PAST MISTAKES AND SUCCESSES

Studying church history provides an invaluable opportunity to learn from the past. History is replete with examples of mistakes and successes that have profoundly impacted the church and the world. For seminary students, these historical lessons are interesting anecdotes *and* vital tools for effective ministry. By examining how the church navigated challenges and seized opportunities, students can gain insight for approaching contemporary issues with wisdom, humility, and faithfulness to the gospel.

The church has faced numerous challenges throughout history, ranging from external persecution to internal divisions and the church's response offers important lessons for contemporary ministry. For example, the early church's reaction to persecution, as seen in the writings of early Christian apologists like Justin Martyr, Tertullian, and Ignatius of Antioch, speaks to how Christians can maintain their faith and witness in the face of opposition. These early Christians demonstrated extraordinary resilience and commitment to their faith, often choosing martyrdom over renouncing Christ. Their writings articulate a theology of suffering, and a vision of Christian identity deeply rooted in the belief that following Christ may require enduring hardship. Further, their emphasis on community and mutual support in the face of persecution can inspire modern congregations to develop strong, supportive communities that stand together in times of difficulty. For seminary students, studying these responses is crucial for understanding how to navigate the pressures of modern society, where religious beliefs can sometimes lead to marginalization or conflict with prevailing cultural norms.

Similarly, the eighteenth- and nineteenth-century missionary movements offer important lessons for modern-day evangelism and mission work. Baptists celebrate pioneering missionaries like William Carey, Adoniram Judson, and Lottie Moon for their remarkable dedication to spreading the gospel in foreign lands, often at significant personal cost. Carey, frequently referred to as the "father of modern missions," emphasized the importance of translating the Bible into local languages and understanding the cultural context of the people he was trying to reach. His motto, "Expect great things from God; attempt great things for God," encapsulates the Protestant missionary movement's bold faith and strategic vision.

However, missionary success often faced significant challenges and failures, which also offer important lessons. For instance, Carey faced immense difficulties, including financial struggles, family tragedies, and opposition from colonial authorities and other missionaries. However, his perseverance and reliance on God's providence ultimately led to the establishment of a strong Christian presence in India. Similarly, Adoniram Judson, who spent nearly four decades in Burma, endured imprisonment, the loss of children and wives, and slow progress in his missionary work. His story demonstrates the importance of perseverance and faithfulness in ministry, even when immediate results are absent.

On the other hand, these missionary efforts also highlight the significance of cultural sensitivity. While many missionaries contributed to the gospel's spread, some also imposed Western cultural norms on the communities they served, sometimes leading to cultural misunderstandings or resistance. For seminary students, these historical examples underscore the importance of approaching mission work with humility, cultural sensitivity, and a deep respect for people. They remind us that the gospel must be communicated in a way that is both faithful to Scripture and relevant to the cultural context, avoiding the pitfalls of confusing cultural norms with gospel truths.

Church history also provides sobering reminders of the consequences of past mistakes. The church's involvement in events like the crusades, the Inquisition, and the support of slavery serves as a stark warning of the dangers of compromising the gospel for political power, cultural influence, or economic gain. The crusades, for instance, were a series of military campaigns initiated by the church in the Middle Ages to reclaim the Holy Land from Muslim control. However, these campaigns often devolved into violent conquests that resulted in significant bloodshed and suffering, tarnishing the church's witness and leading to lasting animosity between Christians and Muslims. The church's past mistakes can serve as cautionary tales that remind seminary students of the importance of integrity, humility, and a steadfast commitment to the teachings of Christ. By learning from the successes and failures of the past, students are better equipped to navigate the challenges of contemporary ministry. They can draw on the wisdom of previous generations of Christians, avoiding past mistakes and building on past successes, to develop a ministry that is faithful to the gospel and relevant to the needs of the world today.

CREATING A SENSE OF COMMUNITY WITH CHRISTIANS ACROSS TIME AND SPACE

A strong sense of identity is essential for any Christian denomination, and the Baptist tradition is no exception. This identity is not simply about knowing the distinct beliefs and practices that set Baptists apart but also about understanding the historical journey that shaped these distinctives. Studying church history is crucial in fostering this sense of identity by connecting seminary students with the broader narrative of the Christian faith and helping them understand their place within it. This historical perspective is invaluable in helping future pastors and church leaders ground their ministry in the rich heritage of the Baptist tradition while remaining connected to the universal church.

The Baptist tradition has a rich history of theological reflection, spiritual renewal, and social engagement. From its roots in the radical reform movements of the sixteenth and seventeenth centuries to its significant role in the Great Awakenings and the modern missionary movement, the tradition has been marked by a commitment to biblical authority, personal faith, and religious liberty. By studying this history, students can gain a deeper appreciation for the distinctives of their tradition and the contributions that Baptists have made to the wider Christian community. This historical awareness fosters a strong sense of identity as seminary students learn to see themselves as part of a long and storied tradition of faithfulness to Christ and his gospel.

For instance, understanding the historical context of the Baptist emphasis on believers' baptism and congregational autonomy can deepen Baptists' commitment to these practices. Believers' baptism, which signifies an individual's conscious decision to follow Christ, is not merely a ritual but a powerful expression of the Baptist conviction that faith is a personal and voluntary act. Similarly, the Baptist principle of congregational governance, where each local church is autonomous and self-governing, reflects a deep commitment to the priesthood of all believers and the authority of Christ as the head of the church. These distinctives are not arbitrary but are deeply rooted in the historical experiences of Baptists who sought to live out their faith in a way that was faithful to Scripture and free from coercive ecclesiastical authority.

Moreover, church history provides a sense of continuity essential for maintaining a healthy and vibrant faith community. The Christian faith is not something that each generation invents anew; it is a tradition passed down through the centuries, shaped by the experiences and reflections of countless believers. This continuity is evident in how core doctrines, such as the Trinity, the incarnation, and the atonement, have been articulated and defended across different historical contexts. For seminary students, studying church history is a way to connect with this broader tradition, learning from the wisdom of the past while also contributing to the ongoing story of the church.

This sense of continuity is particularly important in today's rapidly changing world. As society becomes increasingly secularized and fragmented, there is a growing temptation to abandon traditional beliefs and practices in favor of more contemporary or pragmatic approaches. By grounding themselves in the church's history, students can resist this temptation, recognizing that the Christian faith has endured and thrived through countless challenges over the centuries. They can see that the pressures to conform to the spirit of the age are not new and that the church's greatest strengths have often emerged when it has remained faithful to its foundational beliefs in the face of opposition.

Furthermore, understanding the Baptist tradition's historic struggles and triumphs helps seminary students develop a robust and resilient faith. The church's history is replete with examples of believers who have stood firm in their convictions despite persecution, marginalization, and conflict. For instance, early Baptists in England and America often faced legal penalties, imprisonment, and social ostracism for their beliefs, particularly their advocacy for religious liberty and the separation of church and state. These historic examples serve as powerful reminders that faithfulness to Christ often requires courage and perseverance, qualities that are essential for ministry in any age.

Studying church history also fosters a sense of humility and gratitude, as students recognize that they are the beneficiaries of the faith and sacrifices of those who have gone before them. The theological insights, spiritual practices, and church structures that Baptists cherish today were forged in the crucible of conflict and struggle. For example, the development of Baptist ecclesiology, with its emphasis on the autonomy of the local church and the priesthood of all believers, emerged in response to the hierarchical and often coercive structures of the state churches in Europe. This historical perspective helps seminary students appreciate the hard-won freedoms and theological insights they now enjoy and underscores the importance of safeguarding these legacies for future generations.

Finally, studying church history helps seminary students to see their place within the broader Christian community. While the Baptist tradition has distinctives, it is also part of the larger body of Christ. The history of the Christian church is a tapestry of diverse traditions, each contributing to the church's overall mission in different ways. By studying the history of other Christian traditions, seminary students develop a greater appreciation for the diversity of the Christian faith and how different traditions have contributed to the church's overall mission. This broader perspective fosters humility, cooperation, and unity as Baptists learn to work alongside other Christians to proclaim the gospel to the nations.

For instance, understanding the contributions of the early church fathers, the Reformers, and other Christian leaders from various traditions can enrich a Baptist seminarian's theological perspective. The early church's articulation of the doctrine of the Trinity, the Reformation's emphasis on justification by faith, and the Wesleyan movement's focus on personal holiness are all examples of how different traditions have deepened and expanded the church's understanding of the gospel. By engaging with these contributions, students can develop a more well-rounded and comprehensive theology informed by the broader Christian tradition. This historic perspective enriches their theological understanding and empowers them to contribute to the church's future with wisdom, humility, and faithfulness to the gospel of Jesus Christ.

HOW CHURCH HISTORY FITS INTO A SEMINARY CURRICULUM

Where I teach, at Southeastern Seminary, our mission is to equip students to serve churches and fulfill the Great Commission. The competencies Southeastern seeks to instill in students include theological integration, biblical exposition, spiritual formation, ministry preparation, and critical thinking. Church history serves the students by contributing to each of these competencies.

THEOLOGICAL INTEGRATION

Church history serves the student through a series of engagements with Christians who have sought to understand and apply the doctrines of Christianity to life and ministry. Monumental doctrinal statements like the Nicene Creed did not drop out of the sky. Hundreds of years of theological reflection and biblical engagement, within the context of opposition from the outside and controversy within, shaped Christian language about God, the world, and the gospel. Theological language is the vehicle by which Christians proclaim the truth of the Bible to people. The church, under the lordship of Christ, confesses the living Word. Without serious inquiry into the development of doctrines, students are ill-equipped to address the day's challenges and serve a congregation.

While church history is not theology per se, the two disciplines work in harmony in a seminary curriculum. Church history is not the history of thought or the development of doctrine alone. However, historical study sets the context within which theological development has taken place. No doctrinal development occurs in a vacuum, and an in-depth study of the historical contexts, ecclesiastical conflicts, and political circumstances around the growth of Christianity and the formation of her theological systems and pronouncements are quite important.

BIBLICAL EXPOSITION

Christians do not interpret or exposit the Bible in a vacuum either. Church history aids the preacher or teacher in understanding the Bible, because Christians have always followed the Bible as their ultimate authority. Even when we disagree with past interpretations or applications, we are unwise to reject their serious claims to submit to the biblical standard. Where there is an error, such as "What went wrong and why?," church history helps answer that question so that we might avoid errors in our ministry regarding the exposition of Scripture.

SPIRITUAL FORMATION

Spiritual formation is not a class you take or a series of activities you perform. Spiritual formation is the Spirit's work in maturing the believer. Church history within the context of a seminary is a discipline that forms the mind and heart of the student and professor. Christians have always remembered exemplary Christians from the past as a way to model Christian thinking and living in the present.

MINISTRY PREPARATION

Along with applied theology courses, church history courses do more to prepare students for ministry than one might realize. Church history is replete with examples of both sound and unsound leadership in the church. There is as much to learn from the examples of Athanasius and Billy Graham as from Arius and Schleiermacher. Equally important, church history obliterates the hagiography often associated with great leaders from the past. For example, Luther attacked the Jews in writing. Zwingli opposed the Swiss Brethren. Jonathan Edwards owned slaves. Significant figures from church history who shaped our present reality were not perfect people. Learning from their failures and misdeeds is as important as learning from their positive contributions.

CRITICAL THINKING AND COMMUNICATION

A formative study of church history shapes students' thinking and communication skills. Reading church history to "think along with those who have gone before us" enables us to learn to think like they did. We want to think like Christians. Who better to learn from than those Christians who have wrestled with big questions, faced enormous challenges, and developed acceptable ways to respond? Time-tested ways of thinking, speaking, and acting shape Christians and churches today. Future church leaders must learn to think, speak, and act like Christians.

CONCLUSION

In many ways, church history is like a GPS for theological education. It directs our attention to the right questions, offers Christian answers to those questions, provides illustrations of both correct and incorrect ways to pursue Christian theology and living, challenges our ways of thinking and acting, gives us ways of seeing our context, offers a two millennia of context within which Christians do ministry and theology, gives us proper perspectives on Christian thinking and acting, and provides the foundational grammar and knowledge for Christian theology. That is a lot. Church history connects our present context to Christians from other times and places. Christians' interconnectedness and inner cohesion throughout history deepen our understanding of the faith to form us for present Christian ministry. Listening to and learning from Christian voices in the past connects us to the living faith in which we see and experience God's work in Christ reconciling the world to himself.

Read and Reflect: 1 Corinthians 15:1–10

Prayer: *Eternal God, who builds and sustains his church throughout time, so that the gates of hell do not prevail against her, teach us by the examples and words of our brothers and sisters in the past, and help us to faithfully pass on the deposit of faith which you have entrusted to us by the preservation of your Word through the faithfulness of the saints who have gone before us. Through Jesus Christ, our Lord. Amen.*

7

CHRISTIAN ETHICS FOR MINISTRY PREPARATION

Mark D. Liederbach

Why is the discipline of Christian ethics important for Christian ministry? One need only read a news feed from any major news outlet to find the answer. Abortion, birth control, gender confusion, transgender athletes, "gay marriage," divorce, immigration, racism, war, capital punishment, legalization of drugs, mandated vaccines, end-of-life decision making, euthanasia, and so on. All the most provocative and explosive issues dominating our news cycles and the media we consume daily are ethical issues! And because morality is at the heart of what it means to be human, these issues often provoke our deepest convictions as well as our most troubling anxieties and concerns. Indeed, moral issues lead us to form some of society's most uniting bonds as well as some of its most divisive culture wars precisely because they are so personal.

Consider any number of real-life situations. A member of the youth group gets pregnant. A family member "comes out." A neighbor wants to "transition." A son is sent to war. Someone at church supports a different political candidate than the pastor. A daughter wants to marry someone from a different ethnic background. A doctor goes on national television and tells everyone to get a vaccine. A politician wants to require your business to provide medical coverage for birth control. An elderly grandparent with Alzheimer's is diagnosed with terminal cancer. A school system wants to celebrate "pride month." Like it or not, the friends we make, political bonds we form, and the churches we attend often depend upon one's perspective on these very issues. Moral questions and ethical decision making are the stuff of real life!

Enter the Christian minister—the pastor, the counselor, the evangelist, the youth group helper, the Sunday school teacher, the childcare worker, the average attender seeking to make a difference in the world for Christ. What if each person in our church was trained with enough knowledge to help people navigate the tough waters of life through the kinds of situations listed above? Many of our lost friends, neighbors, and family members are not looking for political fights. They do not want to get in arguments. They are not interested in being lectured on their moral failings. But they do want to know how to decide what to do when they face tough situations.

What an opportunity for the man or woman of God looking to make a gospel impact on the world! Christian ethics finds relevance at the intersection of real-life struggles and questions of faith. Training in the field of Christian ethics prepares men and women to walk into that intersection and lead people to Jesus. It meets them where they live and shows them a more excellent way. It points them to the abundant life Jesus promised to all who would follow him (John 10:10).

In this light, the purpose of this chapter is to suggest four foundational reasons why studying the discipline of Christian ethics is vitally important for effective gospel ministry. First, it is important because whether or not people realize it, everyone already makes decisions from some ethical framework. Second, it is important because behind every ethical framework there is also already an underlying set of ethical presuppositions that every person uses to justify the moral opinions they hold or the ethical decisions they make. Third, it is important because God has designed the universe and every person within it to live according to a good and loving moral pattern. God's story, not ours, is the deciding factor of morality. People need to know this plan and hear this story! When it is followed it may not bring ease, but it is the pathway to fullness and joy. When it is rejected, it may bring fleeting pleasures, but along with those pleasures will come heartache and despair. Finally, it is important because at the end of the day the most important task of the Christian minister is to remind us that God is the center of the story and that we should do everything for the glory of God. Thus, the ultimate task of Christian ethics is to help us turn our everyday choices into moments of God-magnifying worship.

EVERYBODY IS AN ETHICIST

The first reason Christian ethics is important for ministry is because everyone is an ethicist. The problem is that not everyone realizes it. To understand why this is the case, it is important to grasp the pervasive nature of the discipline. Ethics is a 2,500-year-long conversation that ranges historically from Socrates, Plato, and Aristotle to Augustine, Aquinas, Luther, and Calvin, through the Enlightenment period and now into the postmodern worldview that dominates modern philosophical thinking. This conversation dramatically impacts contemporary opinions on all the burning issues and topics of our day. It is a conversation that involves nothing less than God and his existence (theology proper), the nature of what it means to be human (anthropology), value theory (axiology), and the purposes of our existence (teleology). It is a scholarly and profound discussion rooted in a long history of ideas and debate that have taken place in palaces, temples, cathedrals, and the most prestigious ivory-towered universities around the world.

Ideas have consequences. Whether the average person realizes it, the ideas that begin in the study of a philosopher or theologian and enter society through the ivory tower or a hallowed seminary eventually make their way into the bloodstream of culture. This is why those same conversations are also the everyday discussions that happen in dorm rooms, church pews, and coffee shops and around dinner tables. They happen with people who have little to no formal training and often a total ignorance of its long scholarly roots and traditions. It is the subject matter of day-to-day life, pertaining to such things as who I should vote for, how I can earn a living, or how best to care for Mom at the end of her life. Ethics is the commonplace reflection on what we have done, what we should do, and how we ought to best go about doing it. It relates directly to all our quiet, internal thoughts of who we are, who we want to be, and how we go about becoming who we want to be. It likewise informs even what we perceive to be our trivial scrolling, posts, retweets, and "likes" or "dislikes" on our social media sites.

It is important to understand the discipline of ethics (whether approached from a Christian perspective or not) as the realm we enter when we engage *at any level* questions about what is "right and wrong," "good or bad," "holy or evil." In fact, a handy shortcut to knowing when someone is involved in ethical thinking and evaluation is simply to listen for the words "should" or "ought." These words imply moral commands, and they point toward the need for moral justification and/or moral accountability. Whether stated or implied, as soon as the word or idea "should" or "ought" enters one's evaluation of self, others, or society, we have entered the domain of ethics. This is the basic stuff of our everyday lives, whether we realize it or not; everyone is an ethicist!

This, then, leads directly to the second reason it is important to study Christian ethics in training for ministry. Because we are "doing ethics" all the time, the real question is not if someone *is* an ethicist, but what *kind* of ethicist they are. Put another way, the most important question is not *whether* someone is doing ethics, rather it is *by what standard* of evaluation are they doing it.

EVERYBODY HAS ETHICAL PRESUPPOSITIONS

The fact that everybody is already working from an ethical point of view also means that whether we know it or can articulate it, all of us are already working from a set of underlying presuppositions about what really matters in the world and how things *ought* to unfold. That is, any time any person makes a judgment call about whether something is "right or wrong," "good or bad," "holy or evil," that person's conclusion flows out of some underlying idea or standard that functions in the person's heart and/or mind as the basis of evaluation.

And herein lies the first problem. While it is true that all of us function from a set of underlying values, it is too often the case that when put to the test, most of us have trouble articulating what those values are and why it is we hold to them so dearly. This is problematic precisely because we tend to hold to our opinions on many of these ethical issues with great fervor and passion. "I may not be able to tell you why," someone might say, "but I know without a doubt that abortion is wrong!" In the same conversation, another other person may be saying, "I'm not sure I can clearly give you a reason, but I know without a doubt that a woman should have total control of what goes on in her own body." Because ethical presuppositions remain unclear, these types of discussions tend to generate more heat than light, turn into a battle of will, and most often end at an impasse.

This also gives rise to a second problem that occurs at the societal level. Because ethics deals with questions affecting not only the self but also others, it is necessarily the case that when a society determines to put laws in place to govern its citizens, those laws will always reflect some form of moral thinking. Whether, for example, a country determines to allow or limit abortion, that legal process is in effect adopting one moral position or another and turning it into a form of legislation. Again, we see that the question is not *if* some form of morality is being legislated but *whose* morality we are going to legislate.

As soon as the argument is made that one "ought not" harm a baby, or one "ought not" limit a woman's right to determine what goes on in her body, we have entered the realm of morality. As soon as we put a law in place related to those values, we have in fact legislated morality. It does not matter if the law in question is as simple as how fast one *should* drive or as controversial as whether a transgendered person born male *ought* to be able to compete in the Olympics as a woman; we are in the business of legislating some form of morality.

Returning to the purpose of this chapter, one can identify several reasons from this discussion why studying Christian ethics is important for gospel ministry. First, by studying ethics we can identify, learn, and clarify our own moral presuppositions, being sure to align them with God's heart and shape them according to his kind and wise revelation in Scripture. This, in turn, enables ministers to work at consistently applying God's word to moral contexts they face in their own lives as well as the moral formation necessary to see that those moral applications flow from a heart of love for God and neighbor.

Second, having done so, the minister can then seek to help others identify the underlying presuppositions they are working from and then engage them at a deeper level that touches less on the cultural debate and more on the inner belief system at work in the other person's moral system. For example, one of the best and simplest ways for the Christian minister to engage moral discussion at this deeper level is to understand that, whatever position a person holds on any issue, that person will always appeal (knowingly or unknowingly) to some *source of authority* to justify the moral opinion. Recognizing this, ethicists over time identified four types of authority appealed to for justification: Scripture, tradition, reason, or experience. Knowing that this is how moral and ethical reasoning functions allows the Christian minister to move the conversation past the opinion and press the conversation toward a deeper and more helpful discussion of "why" someone holds the position he or she does. By studying the discipline of ethics and learning the cultural patterns of how people are influenced by these sources of authority, the minister can then enter the discussion from a different angle.

For example, for reasons that are beyond the scope of this chapter to address, the minister would know that the ordering of these sources of authority for Christians and for secular non-Christians are completely inverted. For the Christian, Scripture serves as the ultimate source of authority for justification of one's moral position because it is understood to reflect God's wise counsel and instruction to people who bear his image and live in the world he designed (2 Tim 3:16). Personal experience, on the other hand, because it is so twisted by sin, normatively is given lowest priority.

By contrast, in contemporary secular culture, one's personal experience and internal feelings have been elevated to the primary source of justification for almost any behavior. Being "true to oneself" has become the standard of measure for secular orthodoxy and the litmus test for a so-called "authentic life." From this point of view, Scripture is often discarded as an outdated form of patriarchal and paternalistic nonsense.

Ordering of Sources of Authority

Christian	*Secular*
1. Scripture	1. Experience
2. Tradition	2. Reason
3. Reason	3. Tradition
4. Experience	4. Scripture

Exploring these differing foundations for why one arrives at a particular moral opinion and how one appeals to these differing sources of authority can help the Christian minister to move the conversation toward the gospel by simply asking, "Why?" For example, returning to the abortion debate from the previous paragraphs, what if ministers changed the direction of the conversation and instead of merely asserting their own position, they now asked a question like this: "You seem to have very strong convictions about this issue. Can you tell me why you hold them so closely? What are you appealing to as the source for your position?" Perhaps then they could follow up with, "Would you mind if I explained why I hold the position I do and then get your opinion on those ideas?"

Likewise, while a conversation like this with a nonbeliever might help move the discussion to an evangelistic encounter, a similar conversation with a younger believer or a member of one's congregation might help them navigate past mere opinion toward informed conviction. Indeed, it may also help them align more closely with God's grand plan for the universe and his good instructions for life and practice within it.

EVERYBODY NEEDS TO UNDERSTAND GOD'S STORY

Rightly understood, studying Christian ethics is an adventure of discovery. It is a discovery of God himself and his infinite and eternal attributes, a discovery of God's great and glorious design for the world he created, and a discovery of his good moral instructions given in lovingkindness in order that we might flourish maximally and experience the abundant life he promised for us (John 10:10).

Unfortunately, this is not the way most think of—or experience—the study of Christian ethics. For the average Christian, the idea of studying Christian ethics all too often conjures up visions of a systematic indoctrination via Sunday school lists of rules that are generated by cold moralism or rigid rule keeping. For non-Christians in our increasingly secularized world, university professors and popular media outlets often peddle a version of ethics that is in truth little more than a journey of self-discovery and self-actualization. Phrases like "authenticity," "tolerance," and "social justice" fill the airwaves of contemporary culture, but the underlying values that fuel these buzzwords are a commitment to radical personal autonomy, moral relativism, and pragmatic self-determinism. For today's postmodern person, morality is not something external to oneself that is discovered; it is a personal invention of a "designer morality" personally crafted to affirm whatever one feels or thinks. "You be you!" we shout to one another as we shake our fists at the patriarchy that brought oppression to us all in the previous decades and centuries.

This leads us to the third reason studying the discipline of Christian ethics is so especially important for the Christian minister. People need to be told the truth about both reality and morality. They need to hear a better story, a truer story.

They need to be told that the world we live in is not merely the product of random evolutionary processes. They need to be told that morality is not merely a set of oppressive rules given by a cosmic killjoy, nor is it simply a matter of invented therapeutic self-affirmations. They need to be told that they are not merely autonomous decision makers trying to carve out some form of personal significance in an otherwise meaningless universe.

When people live according to the world's false story, they will be told that they have every right "to be true to themselves." They will be given social permission to pursue their fleshly desires. They will get their fill of worldly pleasures. But along with these things, they will get despair. For the simple fact of the matter is that, while God invented the ability for a person to make decisions, have desires, and experience pleasures, he did so within a context of an eternal design and infinitely wise moral order. If one misses this truth, they miss everything.

In contrast, when properly understood and taught, the discipline of Christian ethics takes a person of the gospel on a journey of discovery that begins with a long gaze at the God who was "in the beginning" (Gen 1:1).[1] It then describes and considers the possibilities of wonder God designed humans to

1. All Scripture references in this chapter are from the English Standard Version.

enjoy in the pre-fallen garden of Eden (Gen 1–2). It honestly recounts the first human sin and mournfully ponders the devastating impact this sin and fall from grace has on all of creation—including the people God created in his image (Gen 3). With immense joy it then tells the story of God's plan not only to preserve and rescue his world but to restore it through the great redemptive work of Jesus Christ's life, death, and resurrection (Eph 2:1–10). From this vantage point Christian ethics then investigates with great thankfulness God's revealed moral pathways back into flourishing. It seeks to pursue God through joyful obedience that shapes our character to reflexively worship God in all we do in a joyful anticipation of a full and final restoration of all things at the end of the age (John 14:15, 21; Heb 12:1–2). And finally, when it is rightly taught, Christian ethics unfolds with wonder the hope of finally seeing God face to face and then entering into the never-ending beginning of tasting and seeing that the Lord is good as we experience the eternal increase of God's unfolding glory in our lives (Isa 9:7).

This is the adventure of Christian ethics. It is so much more than cold moralism and so much fuller than therapeutic self-congratulation. Christian ethics is important for ministry because it tells a better story—a truer story—about God's design of the world, our place in it, and the only real plan for experiencing joy. This story is an adventure of discovery about God and his grand narrative of the universe. Christians need to be reminded of it, and non-Christians need to be rescued by it. The Christian minister must learn to tell it well and tell it often.

GOD IS THE CENTER OF THE STORY

Finally, the fourth foundational reason Christian ethics is important for ministry arises naturally from the third. Not only is it true that Christian ethics tells a better story than any alternative, when properly understood it decenters us from the middle of the story and places the only Being who is possible of fulfilling all longings and who alone is worthy of all honor, praise, and glory at the focal point of all reality: God himself.

Consider the words of Psalm 16:11: God "make[s] known to me the path of life; in [his] presence there is fullness of joy; at [his] right hand are pleasures forevermore." While living well in accord with God's design is important, while tasting and enjoying pleasures that come from God's right hand is a stunning gift, and while living in accord with God's righteous commands will result in superior joys, note what this verse actually tells us is the source of it all: being in God's presence! As wonderful as all the fringe benefits of moral obedience and ethical excellence are, they are not the Christian's hope. No, God himself is the gospel!

Central to the task of Christian ethics is recognizing what Ecclesiastes 3:11 (ESV) tells us: that "God has placed eternity in man's heart." And as Augustine put it in his *Confessions*: "to praise you is the desire of man, a little piece of your creation. You stir man to take pleasure in praising you, because you have made us for yourself, and our heart is restless until it rests in you."[2] (*Confessions* 1.1.1). Likewise, Blaise Pascal famously and rightly said: "there was once in man a true happiness of which there now remain to him only the mark and empty trace, which he in vain tries to fill from all his surroundings, seeking from things absent the help he does not obtain in things present? But these are all inadequate, because the infinite abyss can only be

2. Augustine, *Confessions*, trans. Henry Chadwick (Oxford University Press, 1992), 1.1.1.

filled by an infinite and immutable object, that is to say, only by God Himself."[3]

The New Testament is clear that God and his glory must be the lens by which we understand all reality. Consider a few verses:

> In the beginning was the Word, and the Word was with God, and the Word was God. He was in the beginning with God. All things were made through him, and without him was not anything made that was made. In him was life, and the life was the light of men. (John 1:1–4)

> For from him and through him and to him are all things. To him be glory forever. Amen. (Rom 11:36)

> For by him all things were created, in heaven and on earth, visible and invisible, whether thrones, dominions, rulers, or authorities—all things were created through him and for him. And he is before all things, and in him all things hold together. And he is the head of the body, the church. He is the beginning, the firstborn from the dead, that in everything he might be preeminent. (Col 1:16–18)

The simple fact that God created all things, which are by him, through him, and for him, means that everything we engage as human beings must be done for his glory. This includes all aspects of our being—especially our morality. As Paul puts it in two of his letters:

3. Blaise Pascal, *Pensees*, trans. W. F. Trotter, Christian Classics Etherial Library, ccel.org, VII.425.

> And whatever you do, in word or deed, do everything in the name of the Lord Jesus, giving thanks to God the Father through him. (Col 3:17)

> So, whether you eat or drink, or whatever you do, do all to the glory of God. (1 Cor 10:31)

At the end of the day, the fourth (and likely the preeminent) reason that Christian ethics is important for ministry is that when it is rightly understood and taught, it reminds us that perhaps the most important question we ask in life is not "How does God fit into my story?" but "How should my life fit into God's story?"

CONCLUSION

Considering all the provocative and often explosive issues that dominate our news feeds and media outlets, it is not hard to understand the need for proper training in the field of ethics. While this is true in a general sense, at a deeper level Christian ethics is important for ministry because real people in tough situations need real guidance and faithful answers for the critical issues they face in life. Pastors, ministers, missionaries, Sunday school teachers, and laypersons representing Christ in these public spaces and in private conversations need to know how to give biblical counsel and wisdom when asked. They need personal biblical conviction when they face these issues themselves. Most important, however, they need to understand how to navigate these terrains in a manner that maximally brings glory, honor, praise, and worship to God in every context.

In keeping with this, in this chapter we have considered four reasons why the study of Christian ethics is important for the aspiring minister of the gospel. We first considered the idea that by its very nature human life is a moral journey, and that all humans function from some form of ethical framework whether they know it or not. Everyone is an ethicist. Second, we identified the reality that lying underneath every person's moral framework is some set of moral presuppositions that give rise to the opinions people form and the convictions they hold to.

Whether or not a person can articulate what these presuppositions are, the Christian minister is wise to be aware of them and learn how to speak to them in such a way that conversations move past the level of culture war arguments and toward Gospel encounters. Third, we then moved to a discussion of importance of not only being able to place our understanding of morality within God's grand plan for the universe but also tell that story well to both the Christian and non-Christian alike. Finally, we recognized that because God himself is the center point of the universe and the source of all joy, everything we do—all our moral actions—must be done in a manner that brings maximum glory to God.

Building on this last idea, there is one last provocative point that needs consideration as this chapter moves to a conclusion. If it is indeed true that Christian ethics is important for ministry because everything we do must be done to bring maximum glory to God, then perhaps Christian ethics is at its heart a missional endeavor. Bringing maximum glory to God, when properly understood and taught, would also require taking the good news about God's redemptive plan to every people, tribe, tongue, and nation (Rev 7:9). Not only does this mean we tell them the good news of salvation, but, as Jesus put it in the Great Commission, we must also "teach them to observe all [that God has] commanded" (Matt 28:18–20).

Could it be that the Great Commission is at its heart an ethical command? And could it be that Christian ethics is at its heart missional? If the answer to these questions is "Yes," then there is a fifth reason that Christian ethics is important for ministry. When it is properly understood and taught, it reminds us that the command to go and make disciples of all nations is at the very core of what it means to be a Christian ethicist. Indeed, it is at the very core of what it means to live a moral life.

Read and Reflect: Colossians 3:12–17

Prayer: *Merciful Father, our efforts to live holy and blameless lives are hindered by our own sin and our limited understanding of what pleases you. Forgive us, and help us to be conformed into the image of your Son. Through Jesus Christ, our Lord. Amen.*

8

PASTORAL LEADERSHIP FOR MINISTRY PREPARATION

Steven Wade

For generations, the church has employed seminaries to assist in the theological training and ministry preparation of those called to ministry. The church is the bride of Christ, and the seminary has been a handmaid to assist the church in training leaders. This partnership between the church and theological training schools has been healthy and effective in preparing men and women to fulfill their ministry calling in accomplishing the Great Commission. On occasion, and in specific disciplines, the primacy of the local church in the theological training of leaders can become unbalanced. In pastoral ministry, any imbalance weighted toward the seminary is quickly corrected. While it is possible to see the scholarly superiority of a professor who has devoted his life to the study of biblical languages or church history, for example, it is hard to imagine an argument for the superiority of a professor who has spent his career in an academic setting studying and teaching pastoral ministry over a pastor who has spent his life doing pastoral ministry. Just as the study of biblical languages and church history are incomplete without the practical application of each discipline, the study of pastoral ministry apart from actual practice of ministry quickly becomes empty and deficient.

Indeed, the study of pastoral ministry joins the student's academic disciplines and practical application to a ministry context. It is precisely here where the beauty of the partnership between church and seminary is most glorious. For while most churches do not have the resources to focus so acutely on training in each of the scholarly disciplines offered in seminary educations, seminaries, likewise, are not equipped (nor intended) to provide the "on-the-job training" that the local church can provide. Professors teach theory and practice in the classroom, while local church pastors are uniquely positioned to walk alongside students as they practice what they are learning among the people of God. So, the study of pastoral ministry gives the student a classroom experience and preparation for applying all that they have learned in their seminary education. But this training is by no means complete until a student puts it into practice in a local church setting.

This, however, does not mean that the study of pastoral ministry in a seminary setting is not vital to the practice of pastoral ministry. On the contrary, while there is no substitute for "on-the-job training," there is also no substitute for the knowledge and skills developed while preparing to be "on the job." And the seminary context gives each student the opportunity to prepare in an environment where they can be shaped and challenged before they are placed into the actual ministry context. This chapter will therefore explore four reasons seminary education is extremely beneficial for preparation in pastoral leadership.

COMMUNITY OF SCHOLARS

The first reason seminary education is beneficial for aspiring church leaders is the unique community it offers. When students step into their first class at seminary, they are joining a group of Christians gathered for the express purpose of training for ministry for the very first time. This is not to say that there were not serious Christians or even scholarly discussions among other believers in their home church. Rather, when students begin seminary, they join a community of students who are focused on being trained with the right knowledge and skills to carry out their callings to the best of their ability. There is a unique concentration of effort toward scholarly studies and practical preparation joined together students that is enhanced and emphasized when they join the community of scholars with the same goal.

This community includes a group of professors who have committed their lives to the academic training of leaders recognized and affirmed by their churches as called of God to pursue Great Commission ministry. These professors help students ask and answer the right questions in their preparation. Many students are amazed at the end of their first class, or first semester of classes, at the breadth and depth of the knowledge they are introduced to. A student once related this to me after their first class in this way: "I had no clue how much I didn't know." The beauty of joining a community of scholars with professors whose vocation is to know the fields in which they teach is that students are not only trained and taught the topics and practices they came to seminary to learn, they are also introduced to many important issues and questions they may have never wrestled with—all in the context of the doctrinal commitments of our Southern Baptist heritage.

At Southeastern Baptist Theological Seminary, where I teach, professors not only introduce students to the right questions relative to their field, but they also point students to the right resources to learn and study. I came away from my own seminary training with a lengthy list of books and resources that occupied my continued study after my seminary training. In addition to the books that were required reading for class, professors always give recommendations of books on specific topics as they come to them during the semester. These books did not make the list of required reading for the course but are recommended nonetheless. I now encourage students to begin a list of resources that they will read and/or listen to once their seminary training is completed. Attentive students will not only study great resources during their seminary training, but they will also graduate with an invaluable list of pastoral ministry resources to explore in the first years of their ministry assignments.

LABORATORY ENVIRONMENT

The community of scholars not only exposes students to experts in their field and introduces them to key resources to assist in their learning, but it also invites them to participate in shared learning. One of the great benefits of studying pastoral leadership alongside other students called to ministry is the opportunity to engage critical issues in a laboratory-type environment. Remember that, in your high school or college chemistry class, the laboratory portion of the training was meant to be a safe environment where necessary precautions were taken under the supervision of an expert chemist so that students could experiment with the interaction of different substances and observe the results. The seminary classroom is a place where students can wrestle with issues, interact with various theologians, and practice ministry. However, this does not happen in a vacuum. Rather, the classroom is akin to the laboratory in that the students are under the tutelage of experts in the field who are guiding, supervising, suggesting, and warning about the issues the students are wrestling with. In addition, the students are doing all this alongside other students who are also learning and challenging one another. This provides a great environment that employs safeguards so the students do not wander off into heresy or "try out" some new experiment without having others looking with an attentive eye at what they are doing.

Of course, just like in the laboratory, the professor who is offering guidance and warning is a key component of this safe environment that allows the student to grow and mature. There are times when the professor will give strong guidance away from thought and practice that is outside of orthodoxy. But there are other times the professor will allow the student to explore how certain ideas are inconsistent or slightly change other convictions the student holds. This is why it is so important to seek out professors who are unashamedly committed to the doctrines we hold as Southern Baptists. At Southeastern, our professors are committed to teach in accordance with and not contrary to four confessional statements that Southern Baptists have affirmed for decades: *The Baptist Faith and Message*, the Abstract of Principles, the Chicago Statement on Inerrancy, and the Danvers Statement on Biblical Manhood and Womanhood. This commitment by the faculty instills confidence that you can enter the laboratory, engage the issues, explore the way Christians (and non-Christians in some instances) have thought about the issues, and develop your own convictions and practices in a safe place where you will be guided toward orthodoxy, exhorted when you veer off, and strongly warned if you head in a dangerous direction.

However, there is another benefit of the laboratory environment relative to pastoral leadership training, namely, your fellow students. One of the greatest benefits of being physically present in a classroom is the presence of other students. While the professor's guidance is vital to successful learning, other students offer additional accountability and encouragement.

Each semester, the Pastoral Ministry and Leadership class meets in a local church for at least one class period so the students can learn the mechanics of how to baptize a new believer. This practice always follows a discussion of the meaning of baptism and challenging debates about some of the issues surrounding baptism, such as whether baptism by immersion is required for church membership or whether there should be a minimum age requirement for baptism. Once these issues are discussed and debated, the students get to practice baptism. It is always one of the most memorable days in class (or at least that is what students report as I see them years later). The students all stand around and critique the form, the facial expressions (yes, students have challenged fellow students to "not look so solemn" as they baptize new converts), and the words used to introduce and explain what baptism is. This kind of "laboratory experiment" where students encourage and critique one another is an invaluable tool to prepare one for ministry. It is true that you could practice on a friend (as some did when they were kids playing in the pool with their friends), but to do so in the presence of other students training for ministry brings a level of seriousness and desire to learn that is hard to replicate.

In addition to in-class interactions, students often engage in conversations with each other before and after class. These conversations often turn into serious debates as students engage in discussion concerning what they are learning, the beliefs they are developing, and the ministry practices these beliefs drive. These conversations (sometimes more like debates) end up being some of the most formative discussions for pastoral leadership training. And they often end up lasting longer than a few minutes before and after class. Often, they are conversations that continue into the evening and late at night, and sometimes they continue for days and weeks.

The value of these discussions is in the necessity to articulate and defend one's belief and practice. Like any laboratory experiment, one can make assumptions and even make claims (hypotheses) about outcomes, but until the experiment is performed, there is no real proof. Similarly, students may think they have a grasp on a particular issue and are settled in their belief and conviction, but until they can articulate their belief in a coherent and consistent way, they do not really hold a mature belief. It is the discussions with other students that most often force a student to hold a belief, learn to articulate that belief within a consistent view of the Bible, and then develop the application and practice of ministry required by that belief. The seminary classroom encourages this type of engagement and acts as a laboratory where it spurs growth and maturity.

On the other hand, imagine if this type of undeveloped, unclear, and sometimes unorthodox engagement were to occur by a pastor who skipped the laboratory and went straight into a local church. As the pastor wrestles with the issue in relative isolation, he decides to bounce ideas off a church member or change the practice of the church based on his own newfound convictions. Chances are that the average church member has not wrestled with the doctrinal idiosyncrasy and barely knows enough about it to comprehend the differences in the options the pastor is wrestling with. Instead of the safety of the seminary classroom with the guidance of the professor and the watchful eye of his fellow students, in the absence of a people who have wrestled with the issue, the pastor acts in a vacuum to the potential harm of the body of Christ as well as to his own ministry. Of course, this is an extreme example, and the benefits of a laboratory setting where a man called of God can develop doctrine and practice can be created in a context other than a seminary classroom. Nevertheless, the seminary classroom is a clear and intentional environment with professorial guidance and collegial engagement that benefits the pastoral leadership student.

THEOLOGICAL INTEGRATION

One of the weightiest realities of pastoral leadership is the statement in Hebrews 13:17 that those who watch over the souls of God's people will "give an account." This statement alone is a sobering reminder of how important it is that brothers called to pastoral leadership must seek the absolute best training and preparation to shepherd God's flock. Pastors are charged with the ministries of prayer and the word (Acts 6:2–4; 2 Tim 4:2), guarding the flock against false teaching and false teachers (Acts 20:28–29), equipping the saints for the work of ministry (Eph 4:12), and the unity and maturity of the church (Eph 4:13). And these are just the foundational tasks of shepherding God's flock. To faithfully accomplish all that God has called the pastor to be and do, he will need to have both a biblical foundation and faithful practice.

Southeastern intends the Pastoral Ministry and Leadership course to be one of the capstones in the student's preparation, integrating all that the student studies throughout the curriculum and applying it to the task of shepherding God's people. Our curriculum is designed to give students a foundational knowledge of the Old and New Testaments, Christian theology, philosophy, ethics, counseling, and many other disciplines. But it does not stop there. Faithful application of the Scriptures is the only way we know the role and tasks of a pastor. The purpose, then, of the pastoral leadership course is to take the knowledge learned and develop biblically faithful ministry application.

For example, when it comes to the ordinances of baptism and the Lord's Supper, conducting weddings and funerals, or developing a discipleship plan for the church, we teach students that their theological commitments drive their ministry practice. In other words, the way we teach about and practice baptism instructs our people about salvation. This means that the first question to ask is not, What is the most convenient way to practice baptism; it is not even, What is the best way to practice baptism? The starting point is what the Bible teaches about baptism. Pragmatic answers to the questions of ministry practice often leads to weak or even antibiblical practices in churches. Our pastoral leadership course will help students ask questions that will lead them to theological integration across the curriculum and develop ministry practices driven by and consistent with what we believe.

LASTING FRIENDSHIPS

My days at seminary were mostly great (minus a few non-stellar exam days), but I have since discovered the stress and weight of day-to-day pastoral ministry far exceeds that of my seminary days. However, I have also discovered another key fact. The friendships developed in the laboratory of the seminary classroom are often lasting friendships.

I was waiting for a brother who was one of my roommates to join me for breakfast as I was traveling through Greenville.

We developed a deep friendship not only attending classes together or having sometimes heated theological discussions. While we didn't (and don't) agree on every theological issue, we have shared in each other's greatest joys (like the births of our children or the blessing of God's kindness on our ministries) as well as our deepest sorrows (deaths of loved ones or difficulties in ministry). This friend is one of those friends that I turn to in difficult moments to find strength and comfort. He prays for me regularly, encourages me when I am down, exhorts me when I am foolish, and comforts me when I am hurting. The value of these lasting friendships cannot be overstated and are one of the greatest joys of preparing for ministry alongside other Christians who have answered the call of God.

While we regularly maintain contact, it is rare that we get to see one another in person as God has taken our paths in different geographical locations. When we visit, we shake hands, embrace, and pick up right where we left off the last time we communicated. We reminisce about long-past theological debates and catch up on current ministry struggles. We talk about our personal lives and encourage one another in loving and leading our families. He gives me advice for challenges I am facing in my church, and I listen to some of the exciting things God is doing in his ministry context.

Friendships like these are precious gifts formed in the context of ministry preparation and furthered through mutual edification during years of ministry practice. While such friendships are too rare these days, in general, they are much more likely to develop among classmates and friends who prepare for ministry together. The friendships developed during ministry preparation are worth the sacrifices required to commit to—at least partially—being on campus for training.

BONUS BENEFIT AND CONCLUSION

Every week I am contacted by a former student asking for some kind of assistance. Often it is an email that begins, "I don't know if you remember me, but I was in your pastoral ministry class, and it really impacted my life." Now, to be clear, the part about impacting their life may simply be a flattery technique to get me to answer the email, but the student is reaching back to a time of training and preparation to request information, resources, or counsel concerning something they are currently facing in ministry.

One student who contacted me recently requested resources and counsel on discipling and training deacons in his church. Sometimes the request is for a resource, and sometimes the request comes out of an immediate crisis where the student is at a loss for what to do. Most of the time the request is in relation to some topic or issue we dealt with in class, but sometimes the student's request is more personal in nature. I have had students contact me concerning how you know it is time to leave your church or how to shepherd a rebellious teenager. And I assure you, I am not the only professor who receives these requests. And this is my point. One of the ongoing benefits of your pastoral—and other—seminary training is the resources you will have access to throughout your ministry.

Sometimes I simply recommend a book or other resource. With other requests, I point them to one of our ministry centers like the Center for Preaching and Pastoral Leadership, where they will find podcasts, blog posts, sermons, conference information, and other helps that assist pastors in their pastoral task. Or I can point them to the Center for Faith and Culture, where they will find helpful resources on some of the key cultural issues facing the church today. At other times, especially in a crisis, we schedule a phone call or meeting to offer personal guidance. On more than one occasion, these conversations have sparked a relationship that continues.

The point is simply this: Whether it is learning to do theologically driven pastoral ministry among a community of scholars, developing lasting ministry friendships, or making use of the faculty and other resources the seminary offers throughout your ministry, there are great benefits to including seminary as part of your pastoral leadership preparation. At Southeastern we believe in the mission of Jesus Christ, and we are committed to offering the highest level of training to those God calls to serve the church and fulfill the Great Commission through pastoral leadership.

Read and Reflect: Colossians 1:24–29

Prayer: *To the Chief Shepherd, Jesus Christ, may you empower the ministers of your church, who are mere jars of clay, to shepherd the flock of God who is among them, not in a domineering manner or for shameful gain, but as humble servants keeping watch over the souls entrusted to their care. Amen.*

9

COUNSELING FOR MINISTRY PREPARATION

Kristin Kellen

In this book, we have explored the importance of theological education for ministry in a variety of ways: studying the Bible, preaching the word, thinking well considering our history, and others. The last chapter focused on larger pastoral ministry leadership and the need for theological preparation. This chapter narrows down pastoral ministry to the area of counseling, connecting it not just to pastors but to other leaders and lay people in the church. We will look at the state of our churches considering the current culture, what the ministry of counseling looks like within the church, why theological training is essential to counseling, and some basic skills that must be developed within that theological training to do counseling well.

The aim of this chapter is to demonstrate the unique place of counseling as a form of Christian ministry. I am thoroughly convinced that anyone going into ministry is going into counseling; ministers are working with people, and people have problems. That reality is inescapable. We must be well-prepared to walk with our brothers and sisters as they celebrate the

Lord's goodness in their lives but also in the deepest trenches that they encounter.

Furthermore, I am also convinced that the local church is in a unique position to do counseling well. Counseling—Christian counseling—happens *best* in the context of the local church because the church has more to offer than any secular practice ever can, and even more than any parachurch organization can. Built into the church is a community, mutual care and service, regular proclamation of the truth, and accountability. Believers are being knit together and built up into the body as one. And when one member of the body hurts, the whole body hurts. The church must be equipped to counsel well, particularly in our current climate.

THE STATE OF OUR CHURCHES AND OUR CULTURE

Counseling within the church is not a modern-day phenomenon; it stretches all the way back to biblical times. And yet, biblical counseling as a movement has somewhat of a unique history. Where we are today is not where we were one hundred years ago, or even thirty years ago. Today, more churches have pastoral counselors on staff and have burgeoning counseling ministries, which is to be celebrated. But our culture is exposing the need for those ministries in ways they never have before. Rates of mental health issues are rising steadily, including things like anxiety, depression, suicidality, and self-harm, particularly in teens and young adults. The church must have an answer; that answer must also be biblically grounded and theologically robust.

Back in the 1950s and early 1960s, most pastors knew little if anything about counseling or psychotherapy. The culture at that time was one of over-medicalization, deferring and referring to "experts" in psychology and medicine. Pastors were not equipped or competent to tackle such deep psychological or medical issues. Because of this, care for mental health issues was punted outside of the church; pastors believed that this sort of care was outside of their purview and therefore not something for them to undertake.

At the same time, secular psychology—where pastors were referring people—was drenched in Freudianism and behaviorism. Freud believed that most problems in life were due to unresolved sexual issues in childhood. Alternatively, behaviorists believed that struggles were simply the result of rewards and punishments. Institutionalization was a normal plan of care, despite its ineffectiveness at providing helpful treatment.

In the late 1960s, a pastor named Jay Adams began to call out that this handing-off of people to so-called "experts" was not what the church should be doing. He wrote *Competent to Counsel* in 1970, in which he noted that pastors wrestled with their commitment to Scripture and unease with secular psychologies, yet they continued to refer out for psychological care. Adams's premise in *Competent to Counsel* was that pastors had what they needed through the word and the Spirit and urged them to stop referring out for such treatment.[1]

THE NEED TODAY MORE THAN EVER BEFORE

Asking the question, "Why is biblical counseling needed?" may have an obvious answer, but it is nonetheless vitally important to answer. Our culture is floundering as it relates to authority and security, searching for answers anywhere and everywhere.

1. For more about the history of the biblical counseling movement, see David Powlison's *The Biblical Counseling Movement: History and Context* (Greensboro, NC: New Growth, 2010).

Each person has "their own truth," which means that no one really has it at all, and each person looks to their own authority and self-directiveness, which means they're all going in different directions. This is not sustainable, nor is it good. And yet, each person is looking for a Savior, finding (little "s") "saviors" in other people who were never meant to save. This might be clearly insufficient or negative, like a social media influencer or a celebrity, but it might also be someone who looks a lot like the Savior—a pastor or Christian leader.

This searching is especially evident in members of the younger generations, who are searching desperately for who they are to be, but also in older generations, who may be deconstructing their faith or realizing they have had misplaced saviors for their entire lives. None of us is immune to it. And like Adams, we must realize that if the true issue in the heart of people is misplaced "saviors"—misplaced worship—then the answer is not in a social media personality or even a Christian leader; it is only found in the word and work of Jesus.

Our culture is demonstrating today, more than we have in a long time, a desperate need for a good, loving, authoritative Savior to anchor to. This is evident in that there are higher rates of anxiety and depression than ever before, and rates of suicide and self-harm, especially in young people, are increasing with no signs of slowing down. Animosity and anger are rampant, even in Christian circles. Further, slander and self-elevation have become the norm. For a long time now, rates of divorce have been the same inside and outside the church, and abuse has been and is being exposed even within our churches. In short, we clearly need Jesus, and we need those who will proclaim both in large and small spaces how Jesus meets our deepest needs.

WHAT IS COUNSELING?

How, then, do we proclaim Jesus in the "small spaces?" One of those unique ways is through counseling. We might not think often about defining a term like *counseling*, but I would argue that definitions matter, particularly as we seek to understand what *biblical* counseling is. Heath Lambert, in *A Theology of Biblical Counseling*, defines counseling broadly as "a conversation where one party with questions, problems, and trouble seeks assistance from someone they believe has answers, solutions, and help."[2] There are a few key components here worth noting. First, counseling involves people, specifically two (or more) people, with one of them having the specific role of counselor and one or more of them having the role of counselee. There are at least two image-bearers of God—broken, suffering, yet redeemable—present in that space. Second, there's some sort of presenting problem. No one comes to counseling because life is great; they come because something hurts, and there is some sort of need. Third, there is a conversation between those people about said problem. Lastly, the conversation is a search for help, towards some sort of relief or change.

Lambert rightly states that "counseling is a theological discipline."[3] Secular or religious, counseling contains within it theological beliefs that drive the practice of the counseling. Because of this, we must ensure that we are doing distinctly biblical counseling. Another definition is helpful here, taken from *The Gospel for Disordered Lives*: biblical counseling is "the Christlike, caring, person-to-person ministry of God's Word to people struggling with personal and interpersonal problems to help

---

2. Heath Lambert, *A Theology of Christian Counseling* (Grand Rapids: Zondervan Academic, 2016), 13.

3. Lambert, *Theology of Christian Counseling*, 11

them know and follow Jesus Christ in heart and behavior amid their struggles."[4] Some parallels with the earlier definition are clear, but there is more specificity here. The people involved are under the lordship of Christ and should be like him, and the presenting problems are both personal and interpersonal, internal and external. The word of God and the person of Christ direct these conversations in the context of Christian ministry. And last, the search for help has *actual* solutions that address the real needs.

THE PLACE OF PASTOR-ELDERS, LEADERS, AND LAYPEOPLE

A topic that arises in response to these definitions is who carries out counseling. Within the church context, a variety of people might participate. It might be one person primarily or a care team, but most often it is made up of shepherds (pastor-elders or leaders) to lead and encourage, counselors to directly address the presenting problems, and perhaps even medical, social/supportive, or legal help depending on the issues. These participants do not compete; they cooperate. The role of the pastor-elder is to teach, shepherd, and account for their spiritual well-being, while the role of the leader (in a counseling sense) is to support those efforts but also instruct and reinforce the shepherding of pastor-elders. The counselor, who might also be the pastor-elder or other church leader, sometimes acts as a "stand-in" for one more trained than a pastor might be; they carry out delegated shepherding that is specific and targeted. But we cannot neglect the others in the church. The role of laypeople is to support, encourage, and declare truth to one

4. Robert D. Jones, Kristin L. Kellen, and Rob Green, *The Gospel for Disordered Lives* (Nashville: B&H Academic, 2021), 20.

another, to carry out the "one another's" in Scripture: bearing burdens, speaking truth, encouraging, and so forth. The entire body participates in the ministry of counseling.

THE NECESSITY OF THEOLOGICAL TRAINING

Lambert's statement that counseling is a theological discipline leads us to the imperative of training to ensure that we are theologically sound. But the necessity of theological training to do counseling goes beyond that, specifically in that our theory (our theology) will drive our practice. Competence in counseling is moral, "love for neighbor" is imperative, and the holiness of the helper is necessary as it relates to the counsel that is given.

THEORY DRIVES PRACTICE

Each of us has a framework for how we look at the world, something we might call our "worldview." This worldview is inescapable—we perceive, interpret, and express within the bounds of our worldview—but it is fallible. We are shaped by our experiences, including what we have been taught, and through our framework for life, we perceive and act.

The same is true for counseling. A person's framework, their theory, will drive what they do in the counseling room. For instance, if their view of personhood is that people are good, no mention of sin will enter our conversations. Counselors' beliefs determine their behavior, so how we view people, their problems, change, and God will directly influence our counseling of them. To state it further, our practice must match our stated beliefs. As believers, we must be distinctly Christian in our approach. Otherwise, to quote a colleague, we may "air condition their train to hell." We may give them temporary, external solutions to an eternal, internal problem. Theological training leads us to be theologically robust and biblically grounded in our care for people, so that we approach them and care for them rightly.

COMPETENCE AS A MORAL, "LOVE FOR NEIGHBOR" IMPERATIVE

Furthermore, counseling competence is a moral imperative, a fulfillment of the mandate to love our neighbor. It is unloving to try blindly to help people or not provide competent care; the Pharisees did just that and were called hypocrites (Matt. 15:7).[5] While this does not mean expertise in every arena in counseling, it does mean competence. Theological training, particularly in counseling, leads us to be loving and person-centered in our approach, able to apply God's wisdom to their situation with competence and compassion.

THE HOLINESS OF THE HELPER

Finally, it is an inescapable reality that the holiness of the counselor is related to the counsel given and thus the growth of the counselee. Make no mistake, a counselee cannot simply substitute the holiness of the counselor for their own, nor is the holiness of the counselor *determinative*, but a lack of holiness in the life of the counselor will inevitably be a negative influence on those they seek to help. As it relates to theological training, loving God with our minds *should* lead to loving God with our hearts, souls, and strength. There must be a connection between loving God with our minds, hearts, and hands—carrying out in practice what we hold in our hearts. Good actions (counsel, help), after all, flow out of the heart (Luke 6:45). When counselors pursue holiness, time with the Lord and in the word, and their own sanctification, they are

5. All Scripture references in this chapter are to the Christian Standard Bible.

better able to call to mind passages and things they have learned as they help others.

MOST IMPORTANT SKILLS AND NEEDS

Now that we have understood the need for theological training, let us turn to the practical for a minute. What skills do we need to counsel people well? How does theological training cultivate the necessary abilities in us to walk with others through suffering? There are three primary categories for basic skills that are needed in counselors: firm theological convictions, people relatability, and wisdom. Each is highly connected to the others, but each is essential.

THEOLOGICAL CONVICTIONS

Often when I talk about being distinctly Christian in our approach to counseling, and namely how we might consider secular psychology and what it might have to offer us as biblical counselors, I use a metaphor of a four-lane highway with guardrails. Many of my students will serve in a variety of contexts, not just in the local church, whether that be as licensed therapists, chaplains, non-profit leaders, or other counselor-helpers. But for each of them, we must establish theological guardrails, those non-negotiables that no matter their context, we do not let go of. You might also think of it in terms of the framing of a house; we might paint the walls differently based on who lives there, but the framing of the house stays fixed.

These guardrails include right thoughts about God, people, the gospel, and change. As Lambert implied earlier, every counselor will engage in theology whether they know it or not. Every counselor has a view of God, people, "salvation," and change. For Christians, these should align with God's word, in which he has given us what we need for life and godliness (2 Pet 1:3). In our view of God, we must see the Father, Son, and Spirit rightly, in their unity and uniqueness, and in their roles and characteristics. People must be rightly understood as created image-bearers of God and yet who are enslaved to sin apart from Christ. Salvation from sin comes only through Jesus by the power of the Spirit as we are reconciled to the Father. And true change—conformity to the image of Christ—is the ultimate purpose of mankind. We were created for the glory of God for good works, that we should walk in them (Eph 2:10). When we fail to have a right understanding of God, people, the gospel, and change, it directly influences our counsel and care of people.

PEOPLE RELATABILITY

The second category of necessary skills is relatability to people. As we explored earlier, counseling is an interpersonal endeavor, so we must be good at being interpersonal. Counselors must understand the person they are helping, both who they are and the problems they are facing. Counselors can listen well and attend to them well, demonstrating genuine care and concern. The counselor should also uphold their uniqueness and yet the universality of their needs; while "there is nothing new under the sun" (Eccl 1:9), each person and their circumstances are unique and should be understood as such.

Furthermore, counselors should relate to people with care, compassion, and attentiveness. They should have a genuine concern for their well-being, taking seriously the command to love one's neighbor. In doing so, counselors must demonstrate proficiency in self-awareness: their own deficiencies, their own influences, and their own tendencies. Counselors should seek to know whether they are truly able to relate to others well, or if they just think they do. They should also be keenly aware of their own sin struggles or difficult experiences that might get in the way of those they aim to help.

WISDOM TO DISCERN AND TO TRIAGE

Lastly, counselors must cultivate and demonstrate wisdom. The Spirit of God is called wise and a counselor; there is a good reason those two qualities are paired together. Counselors must be able to apply truth to a counselee's circumstances, understand the struggles, apply the gospel and truth of God's word rightly, and discern actual needs versus perceived needs. A foolish counselor should be an oxymoron; no one wants help from someone who does not understand them, their presenting problems, or how to find a solution.

Similarly, counselors must be able to triage. What is meant by that is being able to gauge the severity of the presenting problem after understanding it rightly, then being able to gauge the relatedness of their own skill as a counselor, or lack thereof. Not all counselors, even professionally trained counselors, can be good at everything; triaging is a skill that all counselors should develop and exercise regularly. In doing so, counselors can identify when to refer and who to refer to, while not forsaking their role as helpers. When we take a care-team approach, we can cooperate and get the best help available for those in need. A pastor-elder, leader, or counselor should not simply hand off a counselee and not still walk alongside of them; they are simply recognizing that someone else is more skilled and able to help *in that particular way*. But doing so requires wisdom and awareness.

DISCERNING A CALL TO COUNSEL

Everyone is called to counsel, to do life together amid brokenness, and to seek to help those in need. Counseling happens in the context of the Christian community and is a Christian ministry. And often, we are the recipients of this ministry of counseling. That might be in a small group, one-on-one with a pastor, or through a formal counseling ministry or practice, but there is a collective call on God's people to "bear one another's burdens and so fulfill the law of Christ" (Gal 6:2 ESV).

And yet, some within the church might feel a *vocational* call to be a counselor. How, then, might someone discern that calling? Rarely do we get to see a neon sign in the sky or hear an audible voice; most in ministry do not, in fact, and the same is true in counseling ministry. In the absence of such explicit callings, then, we must balance a couple of things, namely natural giftings, interests, and opportunities. Many people are naturally gifted at relating to others and are often sought out for their guidance in difficult circumstances. Others have personally benefitted a great deal from receiving counseling and they sense the Lord's desire to "comfort others with the comfort [they themselves] have received" (2 Cor 1:4 ESV). Still others feel a clear calling to missions and see counseling as a practical avenue for doing that, or they desire to work with a people group, like refugees, who need counsel. Another group of people might simply see a tremendous need in the world (remember how we began this chapter) and sense the leading of the Lord to meet that need. Any of these are valid and can urge a person toward becoming a vocational counselor. But counseling as a vocation, for a Christian, is a ministry that is enabled and sustained solely by the Lord, not by us. This calling originates, is enabled, and is sustained from outside of us.

As you read this chapter, some of you might think, "Wow! Counseling seems like a great vocation; I think I will go for it!" To which I respond, "That's great, but wait!" Let me offer just a few words of caution, followed by a few more words of encouragement. Counseling is hard, arduous work. I will say it again: Counseling is demanding work. It is not for the faint of heart, or for those who shy away from getting into the trenches with other people. I said above that no one comes to counseling because things are going well. As counselors, we will see the messiest parts of people's lives. It will expose sin in our own hearts, showing our brokenness, propensity toward pride, and hypocrisy more often than we would like. As Jeffery Kottler writes, counseling is potentially the most "self-confrontational" job there is, a job where you must confront your own hypocrisy regularly, and he is right.[6] Counseling also requires time and emotional investment that does not operate on a nice, clean schedule. It is ministry, and often it is messy ministry.

And yet, counseling is such good work. I will say this again as well: Counseling is *good* work. It is worth it. Despite having a window to see someone's sin and despair, we are also privileged to see people's greatest joys and deepest satisfactions as they turn to their Creator; we see people lean into supernatural strength in deep suffering. These are not only an encouragement to our own souls, but they are testimonies to the goodness of the Lord and his provision. We get to fulfill, in tangible ways, the command to love our neighbor, and though we may weep regularly, we also get to rejoice with those who rejoice. The ministry of counseling is worth it.

CONCLUSION

Now that we have explored the need for counseling within the church, what it means to counsel, and some necessary skills, where do we go from here? Search your heart. Has the Lord

6. Jeffrey A. Kottler, *On Being a Therapist*, 6th ed. (New York: Oxford University Press, 2022), 50.

called you to or given you the opportunity to do counseling? If so, or if he may in the future (which is everyone!), prepare yourself for this endeavor. Get trained. Read more, learn more, observe more, and practice counseling others. Specific opportunities may be as large as a seminary degree but may be as simple as a workshop in a local church, a certificate in counseling, watching some training videos, or sitting in with a counselor you know and trust.

Even if counseling is not your calling or within your purview, you can still participate. You can cultivate a culture within your church of openness, vulnerability, and care. You can pray for leaders within your church who are doing the work of bearing other's burdens with them. And you can contribute to the ministries within the church or in your area that are providing resources to those who are hurting, removing barriers to care that may exist. Counseling is a necessary—and worthwhile!—endeavor within the church that can have a tremendous impact.

Read and Reflect: Matthew 11:28–30

Prayer: *Father, you do not break bruised reeds, nor do you extinguish smoldering wicks. Teach us to tend to broken souls and suffering brothers and sisters with the same compassion as you, and point them to the lasting hope of your glorious resurrection through Jesus Christ, our Lord. Amen.*

10

MISSIONS FOR MINISTRY PREPARATION

D. Scott Hildreth

With so many people dying every day without Jesus, is it right for me to take time to go to school? That seems so selfish.

I just want to preach the gospel and tell lost people about Jesus. Do I really need a seminary degree for that.

As a professor of missions, I hear questions like these all the time. On the one hand, I get it. There are billions of people living and dying with unacceptably low access to the gospel. If they do not hear about Jesus, they have no chance of salvation. And, yes, hurting people surround us, and they need to hear about the love of God and the life-changing message of Jesus's death and resurrection. We are the salt and light of the world.

However, these questions also reflect a short-sighted understanding of our calling and God's mission. It is true that each of us has a personal testimony, and we certainly know enough to point a lost person to Jesus. However, fully engaging in God's mission requires more than knowing and teaching the basics. The testimony of the man born blind in John 9 is powerful:

"Whether or not he's a sinner, I don't know. One thing I do know: I was blind, and now I can see!" (John 9:25).[1] However, this immature faith will not sustain long-term ministry success.

The Great Commission (Matthew 28:18–20) commands us to make disciples of all nations by teaching them to obey everything Jesus commanded. Obedience to this commandment requires us to be as prepared as possible, and seminaries are here to equip you for this task.

I am reminded of a conversation I had with a Muslim seeker. He was genuinely interested in knowing about Jesus, but he had a lot of questions. He had been told Christians believed in three gods (a misunderstanding of the Trinity). He had been told that Christians had changed the Bible (a misunderstanding of church history and textual criticism). He had also been told that true Christians followed the pope (a misunderstanding of Baptist history). During a single conversation, this man asked about topics that spanned the breadth of my theological education. To help him in his search, I needed a working knowledge of biblical studies, systematic theology, church history, Baptist beliefs, as well as mission and evangelism.

As we share the gospel and talk to those far from God, we will face more complex questions about Christ and Christianity. Appealing to our personal stories and experiences is insufficient. The further a person is from a Christian worldview, the deeper his or her questions tend to be. If God has called you to take his gospel to the lost, it is important that you are as prepared as possible for the complexity of the task. Others in this book have addressed their specific discipline and showed why it is important to study. So, the question I want to address in this

1. All references to Scripture in this chapter are from the Christian Standard Bible.

chapter is: "How does the study of missions prepare you to fulfill God's call?"

I know that some of you feel a divine calling to do missions, while others feel called to serve in a local church or the marketplace. In this chapter, we are going to explore how studying missions can prepare you for wherever God calls you.

PREPARING YOU FOR THE TASK AT HAND

Missions is our response to Jesus's command in Matthew 28:18–20 (and other similar passages) to make disciples of all nations. This responsibility is not given simply to those who live and serve internationally or to a select few super-Christians. It is the mandate for everyone who claims the name of Jesus. No matter where we find ourselves, Christ has charged us to reach people with the gospel. The Great Commission is for everyone, including those in professional ministry and nonreligious jobs.

God has placed you in a world filled with people who hold different beliefs and follow different worldviews. Many have little understanding of the true gospel. The people you interact with regularly come from diverse religious backgrounds and have various experiences with Christianity. Some have never heard; some have wrong understandings. For others, the gospel is a competitor to their way of life and worship. When you study missions, you will learn about how these differences impact the way others may respond to the gospel. You will learn how to avoid unnecessary conflict and how the message of Jesus answers the questions other world religions raise. You will learn to share the gospel clearly and make disciples in a pagan culture.

In our study of missionary history, we learn how others have carried the gospel around the world. We study about great men and women who risked their lives to take the message of Jesus to some of the most unreached places on the planet. When we study missions, we realize that our ministries today are a part of a spiritual race that others have been running for generations. As we learn about what others have done, and are doing, we develop skills that will help us in ministry. Their stories inspire us and teach us lessons about how to engage in our complex culture.

CULTIVATING A HEART FOR GOD AND HIS LOVE FOR THE LOST

Through the centuries, men and women have left the seeming security of their homeland to take the message of Christ to others. Many left family, jobs, and comfort as they set aside their own plans for God's higher calling. What compels a person to embrace trouble and even enter life-threatening circumstances? According to the apostle Paul, "the love of Christ compels us" (2 Cor 5:14). We go because we have experienced God's love. We know what this has done in our own lives, and we long to see it make a difference in the lives of others. As we study missions, it will remind us of God's love and our role in spreading it to the world.

Consider the message of Luke 15. Jesus tells a series of stories to show his religious critics why he ate with people they considered undesirable. The first story is of a shepherd who was overjoyed when he found a lost sheep. The second story is of a woman whose joy over finding a lost piece of silver prompted her to invite her neighbors to celebrate. Finally, he tells the story of a father who was overcome with joy when his rebellious son came back home; he set aside all dignity and threw a party.

The point of these stories is clear: God loves lost and wandering people. When we seek to reach them with the gospel, we are engaged in the very activities that bring him immense joy. Consider the often-misunderstood words of Luke 15:10, "I tell you, in the same way, there is joy in the presence of God's angels over one sinner who repents." It is tempting to read this verse and imagine the angels celebrating when someone prays to receive Jesus; however, this is not the image Jesus describes. Re-read this verse carefully. Notice the angels are not the ones celebrating; they are "in the presence of" a celebration. A more accurate and descriptive translation of this Greek phrase is "before the face of" or "in the eyes of" the angels. So, when a sinner repents, the angels in heaven do not celebrate; they watch a joyful celebration.

You might ask, "If the angels are not celebrating, who is?" According to Revelation 4 and Isaiah 6, we see the angels are not looking at earth; they continually gaze on God himself. So, when Jesus tells us about joy over one sinner who repents, the one celebrating is the Lord himself. God's love for the lost drove him to sacrifice himself for our salvation. When someone repents and places their faith in him, God's love is fulfilled. He is filled with joy. Now, when we realize what brings our heavenly Father immense joy, our lives change. To use Paul's words again, this love "compels us" to live differently and serve differently.

This is why, at the end of Luke 15, the question remains, Where do we see ourselves in these stories? At one time, we were all the wandering sheep and the rebellious son. But now, will you work to bring the Father joy like the servants, or stay in your own field like the ultimate prodigal son who did not want to join the party?

The study of missions helps us answer this question. Reading about missionaries and studying biblical texts about missions can help us understand God's love for the world. As you study, you will understand the depth of lostness around the world and will be swept up into the very heart of God and his love for the world. Our prayer is that once you get a glimpse of God's joy, you will never be the same. This passion will sustain you on the mission field and will shape your decisions about life and ministry.

GIVING YOU TOOLS TO SUSTAIN YOUR FAITH IN DIFFICULT TIMES

Has it ever occurred to you that missionary success is a divine miracle? A handful of insignificant people started a movement that became the most transforming idea in human history. The gospel has been carried across every continent. People of different languages, cultures, and religions have found hope in Christ. Language barriers, government opposition, rough geographical terrain, and other overwhelming obstacles have proven incapable of stopping this missionary expanse. In fact, Historian Kenneth Scott Latourette noted that Christianity's expansion is "one of the most remarkable facts of human history."[2]

In Luke 24, Jesus told his eleven remaining disciples, "Repentance and forgiveness of sins will be preached in his name to all the nations" (Luke 24:47). This Great Commission passage differs from the one we commonly quote from Matthew 28. In Luke, Jesus is not giving his disciples a command to obey. Instead, he is making them a promise. If you read this chapter, you will find all of Jesus's disciples were confused and afraid.

---

2. Latourette, Kenneth Scott, *The First Five Centuries: A History of the Expansion of Christianity*, vol. 1, The First Five Centuries. (New York: Harper & Brothers, 1937), 59.

Then, at the moment these men and women felt like life was out of control and the enemy was winning, Jesus corrected their faith with this global promise.

> "These are my words that I spoke to you while I was still with you—that everything written about me in the Law of Moses, the Prophets, and the Psalms must be fulfilled." Then he opened their minds to understand the Scriptures. He also said to them, "This is what is written: The Messiah will suffer and rise from the dead the third day, and repentance for forgiveness of sins will be proclaimed in his name to all the nations, beginning at Jerusalem." (Luke 24:44–47)

Can you imagine their confusion? Jesus gave them a promise they could not begin to comprehend. We have no evidence that they even knew what "all nations" meant. In a world without the internet, language learning resources, modern travel, or other tools, Jesus predicted the gospel would reach every people group on the planet.

There are a lot of promises in the Bible that seem impossible to fulfill:

- God promised Noah that he would flood the earth with rain, even though it had never rained.
- God promised Abraham and Sarah would have a son, even though they were old and barren.
- God assured Moses and the Israelites that they would conquer the land, despite the presence of powerful forces.

- The prophets predicted the Messiah would be born in Bethlehem to a virgin, teach through parables, enter Jerusalem on a donkey, die by being nailed to a cross, and rise from the dead three days later.

Each of these predictions seemed impossible when it was first given. For the Lord to keep these promises, he had to influence hundreds of details toward his purposes. Now, we know each of these promises happened just as he said; however, no promise in the Bible exceeds the complexity of what Jesus said in Luke 24:47. He promised that the saving message of repentance and forgiveness would touch every tribe, people group, and language on the planet, beginning with eleven scared men and some women in the city of Jerusalem. What is even more shocking is that it has happened. Through the labors of ordinary men and women (like you and me), this message has in fact traversed the world.

You might ask, "Okay, I see that, but how does this sustain my faith?"

Consider this: if God can influence the course of history to keep this missionary promise, is there anything he cannot do in your life?

As each of us faces the daily grind of living in a broken world, it is tempting to give up. We face problems that seem insurmountable, and our faith is challenged. Sometimes our prayers feel like a laundry list of impossible crises. However, when we study missions, we are reminded that God is both willing and able to keep his promises. Things that seem impossible to us are always possible for God.

Guess what? The greatest demonstration of God keeping his promise looks back at you in the mirror each morning. Each of us are living examples of the fulfillment of Jesus's promise in

Luke 24. When he promised his disciples that repentance and forgiveness of sins would be preached to the nations, you and I were these nations. Sit back for a moment and consider all the minute and major details that God influenced for you to hear the gospel. If he can do that, what can he not do?

As you study missions, your faith will grow. As you learn about God's powerful promises and his ability to keep them, you will pray with faith and live with confidence in the face of life's difficulties.

HELPING YOU TO READ THE BIBLE BETTER

The Bible is a missionary book. By this, I do not simply mean that missions is the primary theme of the Bible. Rather, the Bible was written for the purpose of teaching who Jesus is and pointing people toward a right relationship with God through Christ. This is a missionary activity. The message of the Bible is clear: sin broke the world, but there is hope in Christ for anyone who places their trust in him. This theme rings through each book in the Bible. Through the pages of our Scripture, God is revealing himself and his plan to the world. We have a Bible because God is a missionary God.

When someone picks up the Bible, it can be confusing. It is a big book with different titles and numbers. However, when we realize that this big book contains a single message, things begin to fall into place.

When we study missions, we spend considerable time in the biblical texts. We study the primary Great Commission texts, that is, Matthew 28:18–20, Mark 16, Luke 24:44–49, John 20:21, and Acts 1:8. However, we also study key passages in both the Old and New Testaments that show God's plan for the nations. In other words, studying missions provides you an overview of the Bible and helps you to read it through one of its primary interpretative lenses—God's mission.

Over the years, students have commented that this missional lens gives them clarity when they read the Bible. It keeps them from getting side-tracked and helps them make sense of difficult narratives and teachings. When we learn to see God's mission revealed and worked out on the pages of Scripture, the Bible comes to life. We become better students and teachers of the word of God.

DEEPENING YOUR WALK WITH THE LORD AND DISCERNING GOD'S WILL FOR YOUR LIFE

Perhaps the most significant struggle students have is discerning God's plan for their lives. Our students want their lives to count for something significant. They also want to know they are living obediently unto the Lord. While these desires are admirable, they are also stressful. After all, how can you know? Studying about God's mission and learning about the needs of the world can go a long way in helping you settle on these decisions.

When we read the Bible, we realize that from Genesis to Revelation, God's overarching will is for the nations to worship him.

- Genesis 3: God promises to send a Savior that will crush the head of evil.
- Genesis 12: God promises to establish a nation and to raise up a savior that will bless all the families of the earth.

- In Exodus and then in 2 Samuel, God promises that the Savior will be a prophet and king of an eternal kingdom.
- In Isaiah we see that the Savior paid the price for our sin and made a way for the nations to be right with God.
- In Daniel, we read how God's miracles not only protected his people but also proclaimed his glory to the nations.
- In the Psalms, we are told to be still and know that the Lord is God and that all the nations should worship him.
- In the Gospels, we see that this Savior is Jesus, who died and rose again so that everyone in the world can be right with God—not perishing but having eternal life.
- In the New Testament letters, we are told that God does not want any to perish, but for all to come to repentance and that Christians should be ready in season and out of season to give a reason for our hope.
- In Ephesians, we see that God's multifaceted wisdom is displayed on the canvas of all the nations worshiping him together.
- Then, in Revelation, the curtain of heaven is peeled back, and we see "a vast multitude from every nation, tribe, people, and language, which no one could number, standing before the throne

> and before the Lamb. They were clothed in white robes with palm branches in their hands. And they cried out in a loud voice:
>
> > Salvation belongs to our God,
> > who is seated on the throne,
> > and to the Lamb!" (Revelation 7:9–10)

Discerning God's will for your life should always be rooted in his revealed will. These passages show us the work God is doing in our world today and can give us guidance for knowing his plan for our lives.

When we study Christian missions, we study how God has worked in history and how he is working today. Week after week, we dig into the Bible, stories of missionary history, and the reality of our world today (so many with so little knowledge of a savior). These topics do more than stretch our minds; they also shape our lives and decisions.

Our goal in studying missions is not to convince every student to go overseas as a missionary. To be fair, we think more should go, and we will challenge you about this; however, our goal is to help students understand that anything we choose to do in our lives should be centered on God's missionary plan.

- If God calls you to be a pastor, we want your preaching to highlight God's mission.
- If God calls you to serve on church staff, we want your specific ministry to lead toward God's mission.
- If God calls you to work outside the church, we want you to see that assignment serving as an ambassador for God.

- We will encourage you to consider God's mission as a guiding principle for your marriage, parenting, financial decisions, and career choices.

The prophet Amos asked, "Can two walk together without agreeing to meet?" (Amos 3:3). This is the question we want to answer as we study missions. How can our walk with the Lord be deep and dynamic?

As we have highlighted throughout this chapter, God is a missionary God. His love for the lost and his desire to have all peoples worship him is demonstrated in the gospel—while we were still sinners, Christ died for us (Rom 5:8). So, as we study missions, we learn where God is moving and what he is doing. Then, if we want to walk with him, we adjust our lives. In the words of Amos, we agree to meet him where he is. This decision shapes the way we read the Bible and pray. This decision influences how we interact with others and the world around us. We nurture a deep and dynamic walk with God as we commit to his mission.

CONCLUSION

I opened this chapter with a series of questions about why you should consider theological education in general and studying missions in particular. I hope you see that your investment in these studies is an investment in long-term ministry, not a distraction from it.

To be clear, you could skip training and go straight into the work. But studying missions can help you be more successful in ministry and have spiritual endurance for all seasons of life.

Read and Reflect: Luke 24:44–47

Prayer: *To the Lord who sends his church to the nations, who promises to bring people from every tribe and tongue into his family, give us a zeal for the lost, that we might use our time, resources, and even our very lives so that those who have yet to hear of you may hear the gospel and believe. In your name, we pray. Amen.*

11

SPIRITUAL FORMATION AND PRAYER FOR MINISTRY PREPARATION

Chuck Lawless

I fear my story is not unusual among pastors and church leaders of my generation. God graciously saved me when I was thirteen years old, but no one invested deeply in me in my early years as a believer. My church's pastors loved the Lord, his word, and his church, and they gave me a deep trust in the word—but much of my discipleship was hit or miss.

In some ways, discipleship equaled attendance. In fact, I have elsewhere described that discipleship like this:

> They [the church] had worship services, Sunday school, small group training—all significant components of a church that wants to make disciples—but they didn't strategically tie the programs together into a cohesive discipleship plan. They had the important puzzle pieces, but those pieces were scattered about. Nobody had put them together in such a way that we could see the goal. Instead, this church ... assumed that attendance and

> participation in all the church's programs and activities would naturally result in faithful, growing disciples of Christ. That did happen at times, but it was coincidental rather than intentional. In my case, it only happened so far—and not far enough.[1]

Consequently, I was much more excited about ministry than I was equipped to do it when I started pastoring a small country church at age twenty. I am still in ministry many years later, though, because those loving folks tolerated their young preacher's mistakes and gently guided and discipled me when I did not even realize they were doing it. They, too, strongly encouraged me to complete my undergraduate degree and maximize any future opportunities I would have for further training.

I finished my undergraduate degree at a Christian college, and I followed that by earning a Master of Divinity degree at a seminary. I am grateful for both institutions and the privileges they afforded me, but neither experience contributed significantly to my spiritual growth. I graduated knowing more about God's word, church history, Christian philosophy, and many other disciplines, but I cannot argue that my early theological training led to my knowing God more. My PhD seminary training was different (primarily because my professors took a personal interest in me and my walk with the Lord), but those first years were unproductive spiritually. That assessment is, in my judgment, a problem.

My goal in this chapter is to propose a different option. It is to consider ways that strong theological education can indeed contribute intentionally and strategically to a student's spiritual

---

1. Chuck Lawless, *Disciple: How to Create a Community That Develops Passionate and Healthy Followers of Jesus* (Carol Stream, IL: Tyndale, 2022), 14.

formation. I want students to see how their education can help them grow in Christ. To get there, we need to consider (1) a definition of spiritual formation and (2) the place of spiritual formation in theological education. The concluding section of this chapter then focuses on the seminary's role in teaching and modeling prayer—which is, in my judgment, the most difficult spiritual discipline to develop.

DEFINING "SPIRITUAL FORMATION"

Keith Whitfield and Nathan Finn define spiritual formation as "the cultivation of grace-motivated spiritual practices and habits, drawn from the authoritative Scriptures and the best of the Christian tradition, that the Holy Spirit uses to foster spiritual maturity in the life of the believer for the glory of God, the health of the church, and the sake of the world."[2] This definition captures these important issues of spiritual formation: it wraps itself in grace, emphasizes practices and disciplines, lives out the word, learns from church history, and relies on the Holy Spirit—all with the goal of growing mature Christ followers in churches who reach neighbors and nations for the glory of God.

More succinctly, Rod Dempsey and Dave Earley define spiritual formation as "the process of being changed to be more like Jesus."[3] God has graciously called us to himself, and he transforms us through his Spirit and his word, and his people are to become increasingly like his Son. As children of God, we increasingly show transformation into the family likeness as the Father sanctifies us now and glorifies us in the future. In Dempsey and Earley's words again, "Spiritual formation is

---

2. Keith Whitfield and Nathan Finn, *Spirituality for the Sent: Casting a New Vision for the Missional Church* (Downers Grove, IL: InterVarsity Press, 2017), 29.

3. Rod Dempsey and Dave Earley, *Spiritual Formation Is ...: How to Grow in Jesus with Passion and Confidence* (Nashville: B&H, 2018), 4.

about a deepening relationship with God that causes us to look more and more like him."[4]

Formation is thus an ongoing progression of growth; as one writer has noted, "Transformation is not a one-shot affair."[5] Its goal is spiritual maturity marked by increasing Christlikeness (2 Cor 3:18). We who are theological educators have the privilege and responsibility to be one of many influencers on our students' growth in this direction.

ESTABLISHING THE PLACE OF SPIRITUAL FORMATION IN THEOLOGICAL EDUCATION

As I attest later in this chapter, theological education institutions can, with great intentionality, contribute toward producing graduates whose lives increasingly look Christlike. At the same time, though, I must admit that some question whether the practices of spiritual formation should be part of theological education in the first place. After all, they reason, these tasks are the responsibility of the local church where spiritual training takes place.

I fully affirm the centrality of the church in the process of spiritual formation, but I strongly contend that theological educators and institutions play a role in that work too. On one hand, we have the obligation of helping our students long to serve God through the local church, whether in North America or around the world. How we address the church in our various disciplines will influence whether they will love the body

4. Dempsey and Earley, *Spiritual Formation Is . . .*, 9.

5. Linda L. Belleville, *2 Corinthians*, IVP New Testament Commentary Series (Downers Grove, IL: IVP Academic, 1996), 112.

of Christ through whom they and others they shepherd will grow in Christ.

At the same time, we are educating students who too often have come from churches who did not disciple them well in the first place. These students come to us with a genuine sense of calling but an insufficient background of discipleship. The churches who send them are frequently like the church I described in the introduction to this chapter: the puzzle pieces of their discipleship strategy remain disconnected.

It seems to me that we professors have two options in response to the discipleship crisis in the church. The first option is to get frustrated with the local church's general failure, critique the church negatively, and make sure future ministers know our concern. Should we neglect our opportunity to disciple, however, we risk graduating students who still are not discipled—and who too often leave us with a slight distaste for the church God loves. Our failure to contribute intentionally to our students' spiritual formation only propagates the problem.

The second option is to be honest about the discipleship failure of many churches while also discipling students and teaching them to love the people who constitute God's church. It is to guide them, following the apostle Paul's example in his correspondence to the Corinthians, to thank God for the church (1 Cor 1:4–7) and love it deeply (1 Cor 16:24), no matter how messy it may be. We sometimes must still take the lead in discipling students because local churches have not done so, but we fill that void because we want to help change the pattern. We want students to be more fully invested in spiritual growth—both theirs and those they lead—after they have been under our teaching than they were when they first entered our programs.

Here's the point: the seminary is not the church, nor should it be; we are, however, still brothers and sisters in Christ.[6] Even if every local church were fully faithful in teaching others to obey, we would still be accountable for coming alongside those churches, pouring into students as opportunity allows and assisting them in producing Great Commission disciples. That responsibility goes far beyond assessing our student's knowledge of terms and concepts. It is more than teaching them to know God's word; it is showing them how to know God.

We are thus partners with the local church rather than substitutes for it. We walk alongside the church, challenging and equipping current and future leaders not only by imparting information but also by modeling faith and mentoring students. We contribute to students' spiritual formation even as we are striving to grow ourselves. How, then, do we make this contribution?

PROFESSORS AS EQUIPPERS

Where I teach, at Southeastern Seminary, our mission is to glorify the Lord Jesus by equipping students to "serve the Church and fulfill the Great Commission." We do that by striving together as an administration and faculty to produce graduates who demonstrate Southeastern's core competencies. We seek to help students grow in Christ now so that they might serve him well to the end.

Our core competency of spiritual formation states that graduates will "demonstrate the knowledge and skills necessary to pursue an authentically Christian way of life, manifested by trust in God, obedience to Christ's commands, love of God

6. I first presented some of the thoughts in this section at a Southeastern Seminary faculty workshop in August 2012.

and neighbor, and commitment to God's global mission." As the other contributors to this book have shown, each discipline we teach contributes toward this goal. We assist students in meeting the objective of spiritual formation as we also help them reach the four remaining competencies.

The first of these is biblical exposition. Students must know how to interpret the word and understand its teachings to determine what constitutes an "authentically Christian way of life." Indeed, believers must turn to the word as they seek to understand the love of God, the commands of Christ, and the global mission of God. Spiritual formation demands applying these truths and lessons to one's life, trusting that God will complete the process of conforming his followers to the image of Christ.

Second, students growing in Christ must also understand and apply Christian doctrine to their lives. Christology matters, for the goal of spiritual formation is to grow in Christlikeness. Pneumatology is important, as the Spirit is central to the process of spiritual growth. Ecclesiology matters, too, for it is in the context of the local body of Christ that believers grow. The doctrine of revelation also matters. We find these truths in the word of God. In all these studies, as Danny Akin has noted, "It is crucial to wed doctrine and life—to recognize the unity of faith and practice."[7]

Third, ministry preparation requires knowledge and skills. Learning those skills can be an exercise in spiritual development, as ministry can be hard and frustrating. Equally significant as knowledge and skill, though, is a Christian disposition that reflects Christ. Those preparing for ministry must be

---

7. Daniel L. Akin, Bruce Riley Ashford, and Kenneth Keathley, preface to *A Theology for the Church*, edited by Daniel L. Akin, rev. ed. (Nashville: B&H, 2014), 1.

themselves growing in such a way that their faith and practice attract others, and they must be equipped and committed to help others grow in the process of spiritual formation. Effective ministry should lead to disciple reproduction.

That ongoing process of growing disciples who produce other growing disciples finally requires effective communication. Whether holding one-on-one conversations, leading small groups, or preaching the word to the masses, believers in the process of becoming more Christlike must teach the Bible well. Discipling others through writing blogs, designing curriculum, and publishing books likewise requires effective communication. To put it simply, communicating the gospel is worthy of our best—and believers growing in Christ will want to give their utmost for him. We professors model that commitment as we equip you through our teaching and writing. In order to communicate well you must have the skillset of critical thinking. A good student of the Bible has the ability to engage ideas and then communicate the truth of the gospel without error.

PROFESSORS AS MODELS

We who teach the word and equip future ministers are more than transmitters of information. We are that, of course, but we are to be much more than that. We are to be a people who teach what we teach *precisely* because the good news we teach has dramatically and decisively changed us first. We are to be models of the transforming power of the gospel.

Students, I am convinced, long to see faith genuinely lived out. Long gone are the days when we could assume all our students saw real faith in their parents and their family of origin. More common than we might care to admit are the stories of students whose parents do not know Christ, or who claim Christianity with no transformation. These students are looking for real role models—and they often look to their professors to fulfill that role.

Indeed, we cannot assume that our students have seen godly modeling even in the church that has entrusted them to us. Few of us cannot speak of some church leader who fell into the enemy's trap. Even fewer can speak of someone who personally invested in us, illustrating for us faith and obedience whether on the mountaintop or in the valley. We professors may be, whether in an intentional mentoring relationship, a large classroom setting, or a local church worship service, the closest some students have ever come to a role model of faith. That is a weighty responsibility that demands our own humility before God.

We are to model an authentically Christian way of life in so many ways. Underneath that umbrella of our influence are the lectures we give, the conversations we have before and after class, the meals we share with students and their families, the jokes we tell and illustrations we use, the prayers we pray, the devotions we offer, the ways we interact in faculty/student intramurals, the service we offer through our local church, the evangelistic efforts we make, the way we worship in chapel, the burdens we have for the nations, the love we show for our spouses and our children, the blogs and books we write, the podcasts we produce, and the social media voice we present. With that influence in mind, professor Michael Lawson's words challenge me every time I read them:

> No matter what the subject, we are always in the business of making disciples of Jesus Christ. We cannot escape our responsibility as living examples of what we want our students to become. Loving God must find its living expression in the teacher first, then in the student.

> Or, in the scary words of Jesus, the student "will be like his teacher" (Luke 6:40). If we want them to be filled with the Holy Spirit, they should at least experience the Spirit's sweet fruit during their encounters with us.[8]

Whether we interact with students via on-campus, distance, or hybrid learning, we want to say with integrity the words of the apostle Paul, "Imitate me, as I also imitate Christ" (1 Cor 11:1).

PROFESSORS AS MENTORS

As a young professor many years ago, I was honored to share dinner with Dr. Robert Coleman, longtime professor and well-known author of the classic book *The Master Plan of Evangelism.*[9] He had spoken in a doctoral class that day, and we met that night for a meal. With him was one of his current students who was traveling with him on this trip. I later learned that bringing students with him was his customary practice. I also realized that for years—decades even—he had sought to make disciples like Jesus did by investing in young men on the campuses where he taught. A few of those men, in fact, were now my colleagues at the seminary where I was teaching.

Here is the way I have previously described what happened during the dinner that night: "Dr. Coleman challenged me: 'Chuck, if you want your ministry to last beyond you, you need to start investing in young men now, so they'll be disciples of Christ.' He spoke with such passion, experience, and wisdom that I knew I must pay attention to his challenge. I needed to become a disciple-maker."[10] And, I realized that both my local

---

8. Michael S. Lawson, *The Professor's Puzzle* (Nashville: B&H, 2015), 40.

9. Robert Coleman, *The Master Plan of Evangelism* (Grand Rapids: Revell, 1993). The first edition of this book was published in 1963.

10. Lawless, *Disciple*, 17.

church and my seminary campus would be the fields in which I would mentor.

I have a picture on my phone from our Southeastern Seminary graduation in May 2022. I will do my best to describe the photo in words, but my words can never fully describe the emotions the picture evokes in me. The unposed picture, taken from behind us, shows three people walking across campus with two of us in our academic regalia. I, the professor, am on the right. On the far left is Kevin, my PhD student I had invested in for many years at both the graduate and doctoral levels. That day was his graduation, the culmination of many years of work and the beginning of a new journey that has since led to his serving as an administrator at another Christian institution. Walking between us as we talk with him is Kaden, Kevin's oldest son who has always known me only as "Papaw Chuck."

What I love about the picture is the image of three generations of Christ followers walking together—all who had first connected years after an older professor had challenged a young professor to be a disciple-maker, and just months after the student in that photo had first sought a mentor professor. Theological education was the context, spiritual formation was the goal, and changed lives were the result.

If space allowed, I could write of many professor/student connections I have seen that have grown both the mentor and the mentee in the process. Among my colleagues at the seminaries where I have taught have been several professors who have sought to personally invest in students at a deep level. It is often our joy to speak of students we discipled who have since accomplished greater things than we ever have.

Students should be encouraged to reach out to their professors, have lunch with them if possible, meet with them virtually in distance-learning arrangements, and learn from them outside the classroom. Perhaps God will connect students with long-term mentors in the process.

EMPHASIZING AND MODELING PRAYER THROUGH THEOLOGICAL EDUCATION

I taught for several years alongside Dr. Donald Whitney, whose book *Spiritual Disciplines for the Christian Life* is an excellent resource for Christians who want to grow. In that book, Whitney argues that "the only road to Christian maturity and godliness [a biblical term synonymous with Christlikeness and holiness] passes through the practice of the Spiritual Disciplines."[11] Practicing the disciplines puts us in a place for God to work in us and through us.

Let me be honest with you, however, about the discipline of prayer. Earlier, I said prayer is the most difficult spiritual discipline to develop. We can establish a Bible reading plan, stay faithful to it, and check the boxes when we have finished the reading. We can set a fasting goal and strive to focus on God while avoiding food for a set amount of time. Prayer, though, is an ongoing, never-ending, often behind-the-scenes, one-to-one discipline that requires our speaking and listening to a God we cannot see—and maintaining that discipline is not easy.

Frankly, seminary training may not always help with that issue. Our goal is to help students become the best Christian leaders they can be. We want them to know how to interpret the word, explain their beliefs, guide God's people, and communicate the gospel well. We expect them to give their full efforts to

11. Donald S. Whitney, *Spiritual Disciplines for the Christian Life* (Carol Stream, IL: NavPress, 2014), 4.

their training, and we recognize those efforts through assigning grades and offering opportunities for further study. We are caught in the tension of calling students to academic excellence while also pushing them toward prayerful dependence on God. For most of us, it is easier to excel academically than it is to live prayerfully—especially if no one has ever taught us to pray in the first place.

That is not to say, however, that seminary cannot contribute to your growth in prayer. It can indeed make a difference if we intentionally seek that growth. And, in my judgment, it must push in that direction if we want to produce graduates who love God with all their being and intentionally make time to commune with him in prayer.

When I teach my students about prayer, I define it as simply "communicating with God," but I further describe it as "a cry for relationship with God and a confession of dependence on him."[12] On one hand, then, prayer says, "God, I love you." On the other hand, it also says, "God, I need you." Seminary can move all of us in both directions.

LOVING GOD

As students learn about God, we want them to find wonder in him. We want them to be amazed by the Redeemer. Regardless of the discipline we teach, we desire to direct students to Jesus so they know him better and love him more. He loves us so much that he died for us while we were still helpless (Rom 5:6), and love in return ought to be our response. That growing love, we trust, will compel us not only to pray but also to study his

12. Chuck Lawless, *The Potential and Power of Prayer: How to Unleash the Praying Church* (Carol Stream, IL: Tyndale, 2022), 25.

word, love the church, and get the gospel to the nations for the rest of our lives.

I have taught for almost three decades now, and I still find myself challenged by the spiritual lives of my professor colleagues. I am humbled to work with brothers and sisters in Christ whose lives are holy, words are godly, writings are word-saturated, and passion for God is evident and growing. Their lives push me to love God more. I also turn to some of these friends with my prayer needs, for I sense they touch heaven with their intercession.

NEEDING GOD

At the same time, seminary should also remind you how much you need God. I have already said that the very nature of seminary training makes this task harder, but the reminders can be daily. In a world where believers among the nations would give much to get fifteen minutes of the sort of training we offer at Southeastern, students have this opportunity only because of God's grace. They hear repeatedly that God has called them to make disciples of all the nations (Matt 28:18–20), but they cannot open blinded minds or transfer people out of darkness (2 Cor 4:3–4; Col 1:13) without God's power. Seminary training can teach you about holiness, but you cannot be holy apart from God's gracious intervention and transformation. Nor can you stand firmly against principalities and powers you learn about in your Bible and theology courses apart from your wearing the full armor of God (Eph 6:10–17). We who teach can do none of these things, either, without God; we all need him.

When we love and need God, we will want to commune with him in prayer. Indeed, it is in our prayer times that we best get ready to lead God's people. As is typically the case, Charles Spurgeon expressed my thoughts better than I ever could when he spoke to his own ministry students: "While the unformed minister is revolving upon the wheel of preparation, prayer is the tool of the great potter by which he molds the vessel. All our libraries and studies are mere emptiness compared with our closets. We grow, we wax mighty, we prevail in private prayer."[13] Be sure to keep your prayer closet open, clean, and active while you are in seminary.

PRACTICING PRAYER

One of my goals in this chapter is to help students begin early in their seminary experience to build prayer into their lives. With that objective in mind, here are practical ways to take that step:

1. *Be honest with someone if no one has ever equipped you to pray.* You will not address the issue by pretending to be prayerful simply because you are spending time together with other seminarians. Start by being transparent with your local church pastor but be open with a professor as well. We want to help.

2. *Watch and listen for professors for whom prayer seems potent and natural and reach out to them.* Do not hesitate to take the initiative to talk with them. Tell them your burdens. Let them pray for you. Ask them about their own prayer journeys. Most of them are busy, but you may miss an opportunity to learn if you never ask.

3. *Take advantage of your ten-minute breaks during the day.* I have instructed students for years to use their

---

13. Charles H. Spurgeon, *Lectures to My Students* (1875; Nashville: B&H, 2023), 43.

"ten-minute segments" wisely. All of us have those times, but we do not all think strategically about using them for our spiritual disciplines. You can accomplish more Bible reading and prayer in ten minutes than you might think if you plan wisely.

4. *Pray before, during, and after you do each assignment.* I know that idea sounds a bit overwhelming, but I do not hesitate to make that recommendation. The only reason you are privileged to tackle an assignment in the first place is God's grace, so praying at the beginning of the work makes sense. As you do the assignment, thank God for things you learn. Ask him for help when you get weary, bored, or confused. Then, praise and thank him when you have finished the assignment. It is, again, only his grace that allows you to accomplish the task, so honor him. Let your assignments become a call to prayer, and you will grow more in your seminary experience.

5. *Develop prayer partnerships with your peers.* Find other students who will pray with you weekly, and make that commitment. Be consistent in praying together even if your prayer times are not long. The practice you develop in seminary will help you build needed prayer teams in the years to come.

6. *Take advantage of prayer opportunities with the seminary community.* At Southeastern Seminary, we pray in classes and in chapel. We offer in-person and online prayer meetings each semester. At different points in the year, we invite students to

participate in special prayer emphases for our nation and for the nations. Not every student may be able to attend all of them, but they should not ignore the opportunities. Prayer is not just an "add-on" to a theological education.

7. *Assume you will never arrive.* If you are at the front end of your seminary training, you should get started well, particularly with your spiritual disciplines. Recognize, though, that the steps you take at the beginning are just that: the beginning. The rest of your life will be learning, growing, depending, praying—followed by even more learning, growing, depending, and praying.

CONCLUSION

The world of theological education keeps changing under our feet. I started teaching with a blackboard on the wall behind me, and now I can show video clips and do live interviews using the screen above me. I wore a coat and tie every day those first years, but that is no longer the case. In those days, all my students were in front of me in the classroom; today, I meet students for the first time at graduation because all our interaction has been through online education.

One thing remains constant: our responsibility to guide students to walk more closely with God. One part of our job is to help students develop (borrowing the words of one of my pastoral mentors), a "sweetheart love for Jesus."[14] We want them to love Jesus, to long to spend time with him, to strive to know

---

14. Chuck Lawless, "Ten Descriptions of a 'Sweetheart Love for Jesus,'" https://chucklawless.com/2021/01/10-descriptions-of-a-sweetheart-love-for-jesus/.

him better, to want to tell everybody—from their neighbors to the nations—about him. Through their time as students and our time as their professors, I trust all of us will become more like Jesus.

Read and Reflect: Philippians 1:1–11

Prayer: *Heavenly Father, who stoops in accommodating love to hear our prayers, teach us anew to pray. May our study of divine things lead us into closer communion with you. Through Jesus Christ, our Lord. Amen.*

12

CHURCH PARTNERSHIPS FOR MINISTRY PREPARATION

Chris Thompson

My path to pursue formal theological education might be like yours. After trusting Christ as Lord and Savior, I was discipled by more mature believers. After growing in my knowledge of the Bible and spending time in prayer, I felt a call to ministry while serving in my local church. I spoke with my pastor about my desire to serve in pastoral ministry, and he recommended that I pursue formal theological education. I knew what seminary was because my older brother had followed a similar path: experiencing a calling, meeting with a pastor, and receiving a recommendation to pursue seminary. I followed my pastor's advice, and within a few months, I transitioned to a new season of life in a new city, leaving behind my family, home church, and a business that I had started.

Before online classes, this was the experience for every student who pursued formal theological education, and it is a tradition that can be traced back to the twelfth century, when ministerial training moved from cathedral schools to universities. However, the internet was a turning point on the timeline of theological education. This disruptive force introduced a new way of accessing education and forced new methods of instruction. The traditional classroom, bound by a physical location and a set schedule, has now expanded through online education to allow students around the world the opportunity to complete an accredited degree regardless of their location. The traditional path from calling to relocation has changed. Students now have more options than ever to pursue formal theological education. That is a good thing, right? Yes, but only if these new modalities produce the desired outcome: students who are equipped to serve the church and fulfill the Great Commission. With the popularity of distance learning models, the seminary and the church need one another more than ever for this important task.

Seminaries and churches have a similar task but a different primary audience. Both are committed to equipping the saints for the work of the ministry; however, seminaries were designed primarily to train ministry leaders so those leaders could in turn equip their congregations. The relationship between the church and the seminary is crucial in an educational process designed to equip ministry leaders for the twenty-first century. Yet with more students taking online classes, there seems to be a deeper divide between the seminary and the church. Rather than integrating ministry experience and formal theological education, churches and seminaries are creating silos.

Regardless of a student's decision to pursue theological education in a residential or online format, it is crucial for the church to be part of the educational process. The purpose of this chapter is to discuss the importance of church partnerships in the process of theological education. A seminary's mission statement should answer why the school exists, and its values should communicate how the institution will pursue its mission, but the core competencies should clearly communicate what it wants to produce—namely, spiritually mature leaders who possess the skills needed to preach and teach, counsel, and lead God's people to maturity in Christ for his glory.

SPIRITUAL FORMATION

J. Oswald Sanders, in his classic book *Spiritual Leadership*, makes a bold and clear declaration: "Spiritual Leadership requires Spirit-filled people. Other qualities are important; to be Spirit filled is indispensable."[1] The task of spiritual formation does not begin or end with a person's time in seminary. A mentor of mine served as a pastor for over thirty years. When he would see staff members in the hallway, he would occasionally ask them, "What is God teaching you right now?" If they could not answer that question quickly, he would send them home so they could spend time with God through the word and prayer. He believed that it was dangerous for a person to be serving in the church if they were not operating out of the overflow of what God was doing in their life. This is good advice for people who are serving in a church or a seminary.

As mentioned before, a person typically experiences a call to ministry in the context of his or her local church. A student should begin his or her coursework in seminary in response to the Spirit's work in his or her life. The ministry of the church "is to equip the saints for the work of the ministry, to build up the body of Christ, until we all reach unity in the faith and in the knowledge of God's Son, growing into maturity with a stature

---

1. J. Oswald Sanders, *Spiritual Leadership: Principles of Excellence for Every Believer* (Chicago: Moody, 2007), 77.

measured by Christ's fullness" (Eph 4:12–13).[2] Therefore, spiritual formation is a task shared by the church and the seminary.

A church should be committed to helping people develop the knowledge and skills needed for equipping the saints for the work of ministry. Programs, small groups, and sermons all contribute to helping a believer grow in his or her knowledge of God's word. Biblical systems of accountability help believers grow in their character in the context of a family environment. Volunteer and paid leadership roles provide opportunities for a person to grow in the skills needed for equipping others to grow in their Christian faith. When a student takes his first seminary class, the seminary joins the spiritual formation process that a local church began, but the seminary was never designed to replace it.

A seminary is a unique environment for a person who has surrendered to a call to vocational ministry, offering a community of learning that exists solely to equip students with the necessary knowledge and skills needed for faithful ministry. Seminaries offer both degrees that allow a student to pursue highly technical programs of study in a specific field and vocational degrees that focus on ministry preparation that matches a student's calling. However, a seminary is more than classroom instruction and formal assessments. When a student pursues a residential program, he or she joins a new community that has its own culture. Students form relationships that often endure throughout their tenure in ministry. Chapel attendance and conversations with professors, staff, and classmates all contribute to the learning process, fostering a student's pursuit of an authentic, Christian way of life and love for God and neighbor. Churches and seminaries share a similar task, but the telos

2. All Scripture quotations are from the Christian Standard Bible.

of theological education in a seminary is ministry in the local church.

The church and the seminary must work together in this important task of spiritual formation. This is not a relay race where the church hands spiritual formation off to the seminary for a season; the seminary exists to serve the church in its mission to make disciples.[3] The church needs the seminary so that students can be immersed in a unique community of learning—especially one that allows them to learn from professors who are experts in their discipline—so they can grow in a deeper knowledge and love of God's word. Students need an environment to develop friendships with people who are called to vocational ministry, and they need to develop healthy habits so that they can be life-long learners.

The seminary needs the church so that students can apply what they are learning. They need to be reminded why they were called to vocational ministry, and they need to be in an environment surrounded by people committed to their growth in Christian character. They also need a pastor who serves as a mentor: a person actively involved, interested, and aware of what they are learning.

Here are some ways to work together for spiritual formation:

- The church and seminary can work together to create a reading list for people who are exploring a call to ministry.
- Churches can invite faculty members to teach on specific topics so church members can see the

3. The mission statement for the Resources division of Lifeway under Eric Geiger's tenure was to serve the church in her mission to make disciples. This is now no longer used.

reciprocal relationship between the seminary and the church.

- Faculty members can invite pastors to speak as guest lecturers in their classes so students can see the reciprocal relationship between the seminary and the church.

BIBLICAL EXPOSITION

Seminary graduates should be able to properly and effectively interpret, apply, and communicate the Scriptures. One of the ways that I experienced God's call to ministry was through the proclamation of his word. As I listened to gifted expositors, I developed a deeper passion to know more about the Bible and a desire to teach others what I was learning. In 2 Timothy 2:15, Paul writes to Timothy, "Be diligent to present yourself to God as one approved, a worker who doesn't need to be ashamed, correctly teaching the word of truth." God used this verse and James 3:1, "Not many should become teachers, my brothers, because you know that we will receive a stricter judgment," to remind me of the requirements and expectations for those in a preaching and teaching ministry. When I shared with my pastor that I felt God calling me to pastoral ministry, he graciously gave me the opportunity to preach on a Sunday night. I was thrilled, but I was unprepared. I had the desire to preach God's word, but I did not have the training I needed in Bible exposition that would have helped me develop and deliver a faithful sermon.

Biblical preaching should be central to the weekly worship service, and biblical teaching should be central to every class and program offered in the church. The pastoral staff has the sobering responsibility of equipping the saints for the work of the ministry. One of the ways that they do this is by teaching others the principles of Bible exposition. This looks different in every church. For example, some churches have mandatory classes for anyone who wants to serve in a teaching ministry. Some churches offer specific classes that are open to everyone who teaches foundational hermeneutical principles, although they would never call it that. The local church offers discipleship opportunities from children's ministry to senior adults so they can help God's people grow into the fullness of Christ.

Bible exposition is central to any seminary education. All evangelical seminaries have classes dedicated to helping students know how to interpret and communicate Scripture since this is one of the primary responsibilities of pastoral ministry. A seminary provides opportunities for students to learn from scholars who are enthusiastic about teaching others how to communicate God's word. Classes in hermeneutics, Bible exposition, and sermon delivery help students to develop methods and principles that can help them rightly divide the word of truth. Students learn how to communicate God's word by preaching sermons in a classroom under the instruction of a faculty member. They receive feedback on their sermons and opportunities to refine and grow as they learn to communicate the timeless truths of Scripture.

The church and the seminary must work together to help students become faithful expositors of God's word. Students in seminary can develop their method for Bible exposition and communication skills in a unique environment. They learn from their professor and from other students. However, preaching in a classroom is much different than preaching in a Sunday morning service. Students need the opportunity to apply what they are learning in the church's context, and it is helpful when churches develop at the appropriate rate. They may begin by teaching a Bible lesson in a small group under the supervision of the pastor, but the end goal is for the person to preach on Sunday morning when the student is ready. Seminaries, local churches, and associations can work together to create opportunities for students to grow in their ability to interpret and teach God's word.

Here are some ways to work together for Bible exposition:

- The church and seminary can work together by creating development plans for students and lay leaders.
- Churches can invite faculty members to preach on Sunday or teach a class on Bible exposition.
- Faculty members can invite pastors to speak as guest lecturers in their preaching classes, so students can see the reciprocal relationship between the seminary and the church.
- Associations can host Bible exposition workshops and classes taught by local pastors and seminary professors.
- Churches can incorporate video-based training taught by seminary faculty into small group leader training.

THEOLOGICAL INTEGRATION

Seminary graduates should be able to demonstrate the ability to understand and apply the doctrines of Christianity to life and ministry. I took a systematic theology course in my first year as a seminary student. I thought I was prepared for this course because I was becoming a voracious reader, and I was quickly making my way through the books in the "Theology" section in our local Christian bookstore. However, after the first lecture I was filled with anxiety because the professor, and other students in the class, seemed to be speaking a different language. I had never heard of words like "supralapsarianism" or "communicable attributes." Thankfully, our systematic theology textbook had a glossary. So, to keep up with the lectures and discussion, I memorized each term. I had attended a local church since childhood, attended Sunday school, and was discipled through a college ministry organization, but I was not prepared for the level of theological training that was part of the core curriculum for those called to vocational ministry.

Local churches are the primary locus for equipping the saints for the work of ministry, and it is becoming increasingly common for churches to offer seminary-style classes. I hope this trend continues, and it is possible because of three reasons. First, in the United States, we have more staff members with advanced degrees than at any other time in the history of the church. Pastors are continuing their education by enrolling in Doctor of Ministry, Doctor of Education, and Doctor of Philosophy programs. There are limited opportunities to teach in higher education, so staff members are using their advanced training to offer informal seminary-style classes in their local church, so people grow in their spiritual maturity. Praise the Lord!

Second, distance learning classes (online, hybrid, etc.) allow students to stay in their local church while they are pursuing a seminary degree. Seminary students serve in staff positions while they are learning from trained scholars. This creates a powerful learning environment because to effectively teach doctrinal truth, you must know the content at a much deeper level. This is a picture of 2 Timothy 2:2: "What you have heard from me in the presence of many witnesses, commit to faithful men who will be able to teach others also."

Third, as seminaries continue to explore ways that they can partner with local churches, field-based training classes will become more popular. Churches that have staff members with advanced degrees now have opportunities to offer formal theological training for their congregation because of strategic partnerships with seminaries. Ministry-based classes like Pastoral Ministry, Bible Exposition, Sermon Delivery, and Discipleship and Disciple-Making are a few of the courses that are offered when a church and seminary work together to equip the saints for the work of ministry.

The goal of doctrine is not memorization but transformation. Theological integration is for every follower of Christ. Therefore, the church and the seminary, when working in a reciprocal relationship, can strengthen one another as we seek to build up the body of Christ.

Here are some ways to work together for theological integration:

- The church and seminary can work together by offering informal and formal theological education classes.
- Churches can offer seminary-style classes to help their members grow in their knowledge of the Bible, theology, and church history and invite faculty members from a seminary to serve as guest lecturers.
- Faculty members can create ministry application assignments for their classes, so that students can

apply what they are learning in their own ministry context.

- Churches that have staff members with advanced degrees can establish a partnership with a seminary to offer courses in their church for academic credit.

CRITICAL THINKING AND COMMUNICATION

Seminary students should be able to demonstrate the ability to think critically, argue persuasively, and communicate clearly. The ability to think critically and train others to think critically is an essential skill in the twenty-first century. I remember when I purchased my first smartphone. It was an iPhone 3GS. The primary reason I purchased this phone was to access my email and calendar as I traveled. However, I realized only after a few days how addictive a smartphone can be.

Smartphones change the way that we interact with information. Social media, news feeds, and work-related apps keep us distracted throughout our waking hours, but they are even changing the way that we process information. For example, Nicholas Carr claims that if "you were to set out to invent a medium that would rewire our mental circuits as quickly and thoroughly as possible, you would probably end up designing something that looks and works a lot like the Internet."[4] The smartphone puts the internet in our pocket. A person can simply unlock their phone and access information about what is going on in the world, at their workplace, or in their friend

4. Nicholas Carr, *The Shallows: What the Internet Is Doing to Our Brains* (New York: W. W. Norton, 2010), 116.

circle. The amount of information that we are consuming daily is overwhelming. Access to information is not the problem; the ability to discern what is true is.

Churches are filled with people from various backgrounds, vocations, and cultures. They are united in one truth: Jesus is Lord. However, one recent threat to the unity of local congregations was the global pandemic in 2020. People were divided over how the church should respond to mask requirements and social gatherings. Social media feeds were filled with false information, and pastors were tasked with the job of helping people think critically regarding important topics in health, politics, and the Christian faith.

Pastors are public theologians, and they help their congregation not only hear what God has said in his word but also how they should live considering God's revealed truth. Written and verbal communication are the tools of the trade, but Paul emphasizes that we should communicate truth with love (Eph 4:15). Ministers should never shy away from communicating the truth of God's word, but the motive behind the message is often revealed in the delivery. Ministry leaders should not apply what they have learned in seminary to demonstrate their superior knowledge of the Bible; rather, their motive should be a genuine desire to help their people by teaching them to think biblically about all aspects of life.

In addition to Bible and theology classes, seminaries offer Christian philosophy and ethics courses that help equip students to think carefully through ontological and epistemological questions. They offer courses in biblical counseling and pastoral care that help students to develop a comprehensive approach to soul care and mental health issues. They also offer biblical anthropology courses that cover important topics like identity, gender, and sexuality. Seminaries have trained scholars who specialize in these topics, so they can equip students for faithful ministry in the twenty-first century.

The church and the seminary must work together to help people develop critical thinking skills and to communicate clearly. Ministry will only become more complex as we proclaim objective truth to a society that refuses to submit to God's law and his design. Our calling is to remain faithful to the simple truth of the gospel until we all reach unity in the faith and in the knowledge of God's Son (Eph 4:13).

Here are some ways to work together for critical thinking and communication:

- Churches can work with seminaries to host conferences on critical issues of faith and culture.
- Seminaries can develop specific classes that engage some of the most pressing issues in ministry.
- Seminaries can develop non-formal courses that provide just-in-time training for volunteers and staff members.

MINISTRY PREPARATION

Seminary graduates should be able to demonstrate the knowledge, skills, and Christian disposition necessary for ministry and leadership in the church and among the nations. One of my favorite books is *The Master Plan of Evangelism* by Robert Coleman. Coleman highlights the "controlling principles governing the movements of the Master in the hope that our own labors might be conformed to a similar pattern."[5] I try to read this book every year because I have found that it helps me focus

---

5. Robert Coleman, *The Master Plan of Evangelism* (Grand Rapids: Revell, 1993), 14.

on Christ and his method for leadership development. Rather than developing and promoting a specific program, his method was simple: invest in a few people who can develop others. As Coleman would say, "Men were to be his method of winning the world to God."[6]

Going back to our foundational text for this chapter, Ephesians 4:11–16, knowledge of God's Son is essential for spiritual maturity. God uses apostles, prophets, evangelists, pastors, and teachers for the task of equipping the saints for the work of the ministry (4:11). The local church is the primary learning environment for a person to develop the knowledge, skills, and Christian disposition that are necessary for a leadership role within the church. A person can read every book on preaching, but if he does not stand in front of God's people and proclaim his word, his knowledge of ministry of proclamation will always be limited. If students memorize every word of their favorite systematic theology textbook but they have not discipled another believer so he or she grows in spiritual maturity, then they have missed the purpose of Christian doctrine. Finally, if they are not personally growing in their walk with Christ, then their tenure in ministry will be limited. We must always remember Jesus's words: "I am the vine; you are the branches. The one who remains in me and I in him produces much fruit, because you can do nothing without me" (John 15:5). The local church serves both as the starting point for ministry preparation and the destination.

The church and the seminary must work together to prepare men and women for vocational ministry. I teach leadership courses at Southeastern Baptist Theological Seminary (SEBTS), and I am often asked if we are in a leadership crisis.

---

6. Coleman, *Master Plan of Evangelism*, 21.

My response is always the same: I do not think we are in a leadership crisis, but I do think we are in a *leadership development* crisis. For example, a pastor recently told me that his church has more leadership opportunities than leaders. Unfortunately, this is all too common in Southern Baptist churches.

I am encouraged to see a renewed interest in churches starting residency programs and internships; it takes planning and intentionality to develop leaders, and seminaries can help. Programs like the Equip Network at SEBTS work with local churches to develop leadership development programs, so students can serve in their local church and earn academic credit toward a degree. In some cases, churches can create residency programs that allow a student to receive training in their local context and complete a Master of Arts degree at the same time. Students who are called by God to vocational ministry should not have to compartmentalize their ministry role and theological education. We have an opportunity to create powerful learning environments that demonstrate the reciprocal relationship between the seminary and the church.

Here are some ways to work together for ministry preparation:

- Churches can work with seminaries to develop an integrated curriculum that intentionally integrates their ministry experience with seminary courses.
- Seminaries can develop flexible practicum courses that allow pastors who have the proper credentials to serve as the professor for ministry-based courses.

- Seminaries can connect pastors who are interested in starting an internship or residency program with alumni who are already offering these types of programs.

CONCLUSION

Accomplishing Ephesians 4:11–16 is not just about cooperation between churches and seminaries; it is also about pedagogy. Churches and seminaries can work together to provide a powerful learning experience that will help students grow in their knowledge of God's word, personal holiness, and the ability to teach and lead others toward spiritual maturity. Lasting spiritual change is the desired outcome, and local churches and seminaries have been entrusted with the task of leadership development. We must work together to equip the saints for the work of the ministry so we can build up the body of Christ until we all reach unity in the faith and in the knowledge of God's Son, growing into maturity with a stature measured by Christ's fullness

Read and Reflect: Ephesians 4:12–13

Prayer: *Our Father who is in heaven, may your kingdom come, and your will be done on earth as it is in heaven. Grant that we faithfully serve the ministry and mission of your church for the glory of your word and gospel through Jesus Christ, our Lord. Amen.*

13

A PERSONAL REFLECTION

Jonathan D. Six

I remember it like it was yesterday, embarking on a unique journey. I was attending seminary. I would give the next few years to learn the Bible and study theology, ethics, and church history. I would know the history of missions and my Baptist heritage. I would come to understand more fully my role to make disciples and give a defense for the faith. I would labor to learn to teach the Bible. I was excited to traverse this journey. My pastor strongly encouraged me to attend seminary. I had no idea what I was getting myself into. For the most part, I had a positive view of theological education, except for one pastor I knew who warned me that such study might ruin me and prevent me from being effective in ministry.

I was so excited about my first day of classes that I arrived thirty minutes early. On that first day, I met two men who are enduring friends to this day. My first semester was tough. I read and wrote more than expected, but this preparation was different. I enjoyed all of the work I was doing and had a new drive to work hard and learn all I could. Throughout my seminary journey, the Lord blessed me with incredible faculty and great mentors to help maximize my preparation.

The first lesson I learned was to see my seminary training as a once-in-a-lifetime experience. I was not just adding my training to everything else, but this was one time in my life when I would wholly dedicate myself to ministry preparation. I would have many years to serve in vocational or bi-vocational ministry, but I only had a small window to prepare. I wanted to reorient my life around my preparation. To this day, I remind students that it is okay to reorient your life around ministry preparation for a time. If you have a family, learn to balance excellence at home and in the classroom. Do not sacrifice being a spouse or a parent for a grade. Be willing to give it your all, but do not idolize your seminary grades.

One of my greatest joys in seminary was getting to know faculty members. I sought to learn from faculty both in the classroom and church, and I sought every opportunity I could get. In my experience, faculty want to build relationships with students and provide mentorship that supports what the student learns in the classroom. I cannot encourage you strongly enough to seek out mentorship relationships with the faculty who teach you.

A colleague once gave me the valuable advice to take faculty, not classes. This means that you should strive to find those faculty members with whom you learn best and take as many of their classes as possible. Often, students will take the classes that are available with little regard for who will teach them. Every student learns differently. Find the faculty member who helps facilitate your growth and learning the best.

The most important task for new students is finding and joining a local church. The local church supplements and supports the seminary student by providing a laboratory for what you learn in the classroom. Just a warning: join a church to learn to be a church member first. Too many seminary students assume they are now experts and arrogantly go to churches to fix everything wrong. Learn to be a faithful member who practices what you learn in the classroom.

One of the more difficult lessons for me in seminary was cultivating the discipline to read the Bible and pray. I often thought that my reading of a theology text could replace my reading of the Bible. Do not get caught in this trap. Sure, an excellent theology text should lead you to awe and worship of the Lord, but it should never replace the word of God. Develop the discipline to regularly read the Bible and pray as an act of worship to the Lord.

In conclusion, I want to offer practical advice to help you prepare for your seminary journey. First, learn to read effectively and efficiently. You will need to read many books and do so well. Get *How to Read a Book* by Mortimer Adler and Charles Van Doren. This book is valuable for learning to read the right way.

Learn to write. I never learned to write in college, and seminary was challenging. I still remember feedback from one of my papers: "Jonathan, your sentences are like square wheels on a car. They will get you there, but it will be a bumpy ride along the way." Read the feedback you receive from your professors and seek out trusted friends to give you constructive feedback on your assignments. Good feedback will help you develop as a writer. Also, use research tools in the library and writing centers to help you learn to write excellently.

Work hard to ensure that your love for Christ, his church, and his mission only grows during your ministry preparation. *Soli Deo Gloria*!

BIBLIOGRAPHY

Akin, Daniel L. *A Theology for the Church*. Nashville: B&H Academic, 2014.

Coleman, Robert E. *The Master Plan of Evangelism*. Grand Rapids: Revell, 1993.

Hardy, H. H., II. *Exegetical Gems from Biblical Hebrew: A Refreshing Guide to Grammar and Interpretation*. Grand Rapids: Baker Academic, 2019.

Hildreth, D. Scott. *Together on God's Mission: How Southern Baptists Cooperate to Fulfill the Great Commission*. Nashville: B&H, 2018.

Inman, Ross D. *Christian Philosophy as a Way of Life: An Invitation to Wonder*. Grand Rapids: Baker Academic, 2023.

Jones, Robert D., Kristin L. Kellen, and Rob Green. *The Gospel for Disordered Lives: An Introduction to Christ-Centered Biblical Counseling*. Nashville: B&H Academic, 2021.

Lawless, Chuck. *Disciple: How to Create a Community That Develops Passionate and Healthy Followers of Jesus*. Carol Stream, IL: Tyndale, 2022.

Lawless, Chuck. *The Potential and Power of Prayer: How to Unleash the Praying Church*. Carol Stream, IL: Tyndale, 2022.

Liederbach, Mark D., and Evan Lenow. *Ethics as Worship: The Pursuit of Moral Discipleship*. Phillipsburg: P&R Publishing, 2021.

Merkle, Benjamin L. *Exegetical Gems from Biblical Greek: A Refreshing Guide to Grammar and Interpretation*. Grand Rapids: Baker Academic, 2019.

Merkle, Benjamin L., and Robert L. Plummer. *Greek for Life: Strategies for Learning, Retaining, and Reviving New Testament Greek*. Grand Rapids: Baker Academic, 2017.

Moreland, J. P., and William Lane Craig. *Philosophical Foundations for a Christian Worldview*. 2nd ed. Downers Grove, IL: IVP Academic, 2017.

Pace, R. Scott, and Shane Pruitt. *Calling Out the Called*. Nashville: B&H, 2022.

Pace, R. Scott, and Jim Shaddix. *Expositional Leadership: Shepherding God's People from the Pulpit*. Carol Stream, IL: Crossway, 2024.

Shaddix, Jim, and Jerry Vines. *Power in the Pulpit: How to Prepare and Deliver Expository Sermons*. Rev. ed. Chicago: Moody Publishers, 2017.

Spurgeon, Charles H. *Lectures to My Students*. 1875; Nashville: B&H, 2023.